ALTAR AND SCREEN IN WINCHESTER CATHEDRAL

SOME NOTABLE ALTARS

IN

THE CHURCH OF ENGLAND

AND

THE AMERICAN EPISCOPAL CHURCH

BY

REV. JOHN WRIGHT, D.D., LL.D.

RECTOR OF ST. PAUL'S CHURCH, ST. PAUL, MINN.
AUTHOR OF "EARLY BIBLES OF AMERICA," "HISTORIC BIBLES IN AMERICA,"
"EARLY PRAYER BOOKS OF AMERICA," ETC.

WITH ONE HUNDRED AND FOURTEEN FULL-PAGE PLATES

WIPF & STOCK · Eugene, Oregon

Wipf and Stock Publishers
199 W 8th Ave, Suite 3
Eugene, OR 97401

Some Notable Altars
In the Church of England and the American Episcopal Church
By Wright, John
Softcover ISBN-13: 978-1-6667-3355-6
Hardcover ISBN-13: 978-1-6667-2828-6
Publication date 8/5/2021
Previously published by The Macmillan Company, 1908

This edition is a scanned facsimile of the original edition published in 1908.

PREFACE

THIS book does not attempt to give a complete set of views of Altars. Only a few have been selected which are regarded as commendable from their striking appearance, their excellency of treatment, or because they are the special work of well-known architects and builders. An effort has been made to present as much variety as possible, so that the clergy who have in anticipation the building of new Altars, or the enrichment of old ones, may get suggestions. Not only the more expensive Altars have been reproduced, but also those that have been erected at a moderate expenditure. The cost of each has been given where the information was obtainable, though in some cases there was uncertainty on this point, and in others the cost was not for publication.

By reason of a cultivation of ecclesiastical adornment through centuries of experience, wealth, and devotion, the Cathedrals and parish Churches of England have attained a high place in the world of sacred art. The American Episcopal Church has given only through the past one hundred years any attention to Church enrichment and her limitations have been many. Notwithstanding this, her art creations have not been without merit and her Church architects have taken a foremost place. The descriptive text has been drawn from every available source, such as the reports of architects, builders, Vicars, and Rectors. Several visits to England helped by the way of study and observation.

A few examples have been given of unrestored English Screens as showing the devastation wrought by vandal hands at the Reformation. It is a pleasure to note in the restored work that the prejudice against the Crucifix as the emblem of our salvation is passing away. The late Most Rev. Frederick Temple, D.D., the Primate of England, once said: "I fail to understand how it can be considered compatible with the principles of the Reformation to draw nice distinctions between the figure of Our Lord crucified and the figure of Our Lord ascending, and to say that one tends to idolatry and the other not. Such subtleties savor of Rabbinical distinctions."

THE SIGNIFICANCE OF THE ALTAR

The Holy Communion is the great central act of worship in the Christian Church, and the only form which Our Divine Master directly commanded to be observed. Its value and importance cannot therefore be underrated. Associated with it is the Altar, without which a Church building has no meaning. It is inconsistent to see lofty spires, mighty buttresses, graceful arches, sculptured doors, ornate cornices, stained-glass windows, rich in artistic effect, and then to find the Altar an obscure and depressing structure, bare and unadorned, and utterly out of keeping with the rest of the Church, as much as to say that God was to be honored everywhere except upon his own earthly throne. All this is putting lack of beauty and dignity in the wrong place, and relegating the Blessed Sacrament to ordinary surroundings. The late Bishop Nicholson of Milwaukee once said: "Build the Altar first and then the rest of the Church around it." Herein is a great truth that clergy and people, architects and builders, should lay to heart. Better to have a richly adorned Altar with a plain Church about it than the reverse. Make the Altar lofty and majestic that the congregation may be taught to look up to it. Make it so attractive and prominent that it will be the first thing to catch the eye on crossing the threshold of the Church, and emphasize and teach the glories of the Incarnation. Therefore, summon to your aid rich and valuable marbles, rare and costly work, the skill of the sculptor, the brush of the painter, and all that human ingenuity and skill can devise to make the Altar glorious. Make it beautiful, not for the sake of beauty, not that it may please the fancy, not to gratify the æsthetic taste, but solely and always to the honor of God. To him we consecrate our treasures, especially in that place which Christ hallows by his loving Presence.

> " 'Tis for Thee we bid the Frontal
>   Its embroidered wealth unfold,
>   'Tis for Thee we deck the Reredos
>   With the colors and the gold."

ILLUSTRATIONS OF ENGLISH ALTARS

Winchester Cathedral	*Frontispiece*
	PAGE
Ely Cathedral	6
Salisbury Cathedral	9
Exeter Cathedral	12
Gloucester Cathedral	15
Rochester Cathedral	18
York Cathedral	21
Worcester Cathedral	24
Truro Cathedral	27
Lichfield Cathedral	32
Manchester Cathedral	35
Peterborough Cathedral	38
Hereford Cathedral	41
Cathedral of St. Alban	44
Chester Cathedral	48
Bristol Cathedral	51
Christ Church Cathedral, Oxford	54
Durham Cathedral	57
Chichester Cathedral	60
Cathedral of St. Nicholas, Newcastle-on-Tyne	63
St. Paul's Cathedral, London	67
Cathedral Church of the Saviour, Southwark, London	71
Westminster Abbey	75
Church of St. Alban the Martyr, London	78
St. Paul's Church, Knightsbridge, London	81
St. Stephen's Church, Kensington, London	84
Church of the Holy Redeemer, London	87
Church of St. John the Divine, London	90
St. Mary's Church, Soho, London	94
St. Agnes' Church, London	97
St. Barnabas' Church, London	100
St. John's Church, Hackney, London	103
St. Giles' Church, London	107
Old St. Pancras Church, London	110
St. Mary's Church, Primrose Hill, London	114
St. Anne's Church, Eastbourne	117
St. Mary's Church, Cuddington	120

ILLUSTRATIONS

	PAGE
St. Cuthbert's Church, Newcastle-on-Tyne	123
Chapel of Marlborough College	126
Chapel of Jesus College, Oxford	129
Chapel of All Souls' College, Oxford	132
Chapel of Magdalen College, Oxford	135
Chapel of New College, Oxford	138
Chapel of Winchester College	141
Chapel of St. John's College, Hurstpierpont	144
Chapel of Cheltenham College	150
St. George's Chapel, Windsor	154
St. Matthew's Church, Northampton	157
Beverley Minster	160
Christ Church Priory	171
St. Margaret's Chapel, East Grinstead	174
St. Stephen's Church, Clewer	177
St. Margaret's Church, King's Lynn	180
Church of St. Mary Magdalene, Elmstone	183
Christ Church, Bristol	187
St. Paul's Church, Clifton, Bristol	190
St. Mary's Church, Redcliffe, Bristol	193
St. Chad's Church, Haggerston	196
St. Mary's Church, Marsh Gibbon	199
St. Peter's Chapel of Burford Church	202
Minster Lovell, Witney	205
St. Mary's Church, Witney	208
Church of St. John the Baptist, Cirencester	211
Holy Trinity Church, Watermoor	214
Church of St. John the Baptist, Summertown	217
All Saints' Church, Evesham	220
St. Mary's Church, Streatley	223
All Saints' Church, Richard's Castle, Ludlow	226
Christ Church, Reading	229

ILLUSTRATIONS OF AMERICAN ALTARS

Cathedral of St. John the Divine, New York City	232
Christ Church Cathedral, Louisville, Ky.	235
All Saints' Cathedral, Milwaukee, Wis.	238
Cathedral of St. John, Quincy, Ill.	241
Trinity Church, New York City	246
Trinity Chapel, New York City	252
Church of the Transfiguration, New York City	255
St. Ignatius' Church, New York City	258
Chapel in Church of the Incarnation, New York City	261

ILLUSTRATIONS

	PAGE
Church of St. Edward the Martyr, New York City	264
Church of Zion and St. Timothy, New York City	267
Chapel of the General Theological Seminary, New York City	270
St. James' Church, Philadelphia	273
St. Stephen's Church, Philadelphia	276
St. Elizabeth's Church, Philadelphia	279
Church of the Saviour, West Philadelphia	282
St. Mary's Church, West Philadelphia	286
St. Timothy's Church, Philadelphia	289
St. Luke's Church, Germantown	292
St. Peter's Church, Germantown	295
Grace Church, Baltimore	298
Church of the Epiphany, Washington, D.C.	301
St. Paul's Church, Washington, D.C.	304
Emmanuel Church, Boston	307
Church of the Advent, Boston	310
All Saints' Church, Dorchester	313
Christ Church, New Haven, Conn.	316
Church of the Holy Trinity, Middletown, Conn.	319
Grace Church, Windsor, Conn.	322
St. John's Church, Stamford, Conn.	325
Trinity Church, Torrington, Conn.	328
Chapel of St. Paul's School, Concord, N.H.	331
St. Stephen's Church, Providence, R.I.	334
St. Paul's Church, Chattanooga, Tenn.	339
St. Michael's and All Angels' Church, Anniston, Ala.	342
St. Luke's Church, Scranton, Pa.	345
Trinity Church, Geneva, N.Y.	348
Chapel of Convent of St. Mary, Peekskill, N.Y.	351
Church of the Ascension, Chicago, Ill.	354
Convent of the Nativity, Fond du Lac, Wis.	357
St. Mary's Church, Kansas City, Mo.	360
Grace Church, Utica, N.Y.	364
St. John's American Church, Dresden, Germany	367
St. Mark's Church, Philadelphia	370
Church of St. John the Evangelist, St. Paul, Minn.	379

THE CATHEDRAL CHURCH OF THE HOLY AND INDIVISIBLE TRINITY, WINCHESTER

THE great Reredos is supposed to date from the fifteenth century and like others in England suffered from destructive hands during Reformation times. The High Altar is elevated above the floor of the nave by nineteen steps, which adds greatly to the general effectiveness of both Altar and Reredos. The original work has been attributed to Cardinal Beaufort, Bishop Fox, and Prior Silkstede, though no records or inscriptions are extant in confirmation of these conjectures. The oil painting by Benjamin West, known as "The Raising of Lazarus," hung until 1899 directly over the Altar. A wooden canopy decorated with gold covered the central part of the screen before 1818. In his *Cathedral Church of Winchester* Philip W. Sergeant writes: "The Reredos is so large that it occupies the whole of the space between the choir piers, and, being constructed of a very white stone, is the prominent feature of the choir. The work is very elaborate, the whole Screen being arranged in three tiers with canopied niches containing eighteen large statues, while smaller figures — kings, saints, angels, etc. — occupy the splays between. The pinnacles are pierced and crocketed, and there is a central projecting canopy over the place of the original crucifix. On either side of the High Altar is a door leading to the feretory at the back of the Reredos, and these have in their four spandrels interesting groups of fifteenth-century sculpture, representing various scenes in the life of the Virgin, the Annunciation, and the Visitation of St. Elizabeth, still showing traces of color. The fact that these carvings have escaped destruction, just as the lower tier at Christchurch escaped, is only to be explained on the assumption that they were hidden behind some paneling, since removed, for of all images which provoked iconoclastic fury, those representing the Virgin were the most certain to be attacked. The whole is crowned by a triple frieze of leaves, Tudor roses, and quatrefoils, at a height little short of the corbels which support the arches of the roof. The eighteen larger statues were, and are now, since the restoration of the Reredos, arranged in the following order: In the uppermost tier, to the left and right of the head of the cross, were St. Peter and St. Paul, who were the patron saints of the Church. Two on either side of these were the four Latin Doctors, St. Augustine, St. Gregory, St. Jerome, and St. Ambrose." The writer then states on the authority of Dean Kitchin that below the figures of the Latin Fathers we had two local Bishops, St. Birinus, the first occupant of the see, and St. Swithun, patron saint of the Church. Beyond these, over the two doors, were St. Benedict and St. Giles. Mr. Sergeant then proceeds to say: "Outermost on this tier stand the statues of the two deacons, St. Stephen and St. Lawrence. In the lowest tier, on either side of the altar, stand St. Hedda and St. Ethelwolf, two of the most famous Anglo-Saxon Bishops of the see of Winchester. Next these saints there is the doorway on either side, and beyond these doors are statues of King Edward the Confessor and St. Edmund the King. Between the figures of St. Swithun and St. Birinus stand statues of the Virgin and St. John, while above the arms of the cross are the four Archangels, Uriel, Gabriel, Michael, and Raphael. In all there are now fifty-six statues on the screen, the smaller figures including famous kings, bishops, women, and a representation of Izaak Walton. Above the Altar it is said there was once 'a table of images of silver and gilt garnished with stones.' These images are conjectured to have represented Christ and his disciples, possibly at the Last Supper, but no traces remain of them. From 1782 till 1899 West's picture, 'The Raising of Lazarus,' now in the South Transept, hung here. The place is now more happily occupied by a representation of the Incarnation. The most recent feature of the Screen is the great central figure of Christ crucified, the gift of Canon Valpy and the work of Messrs. Farmer and Brindley. The final restoration of the Screen by the filling of the space left vacant for three centuries was commemorated by a solemn dedication service held at the Cathedral on March 24, 1899."[1]

---

[1] The Cathedral Church of Winchester. A description of its fabric and a brief history of the Episcopal see, pp. 56-61.

THE CATHEDRAL CHURCH OF ETHELDREDA, ELY

THE following description was written by the Clerk of the works at the time of the interior improvements of the Cathedral: "The Reredos was erected by John Dunn Gardner, Esq., of Chatteris, in the Isle of Ely, as an offering of affection to the memory of a beloved wife who died in the flower of her age; it comprises a centre, the front being built with alabaster or Derbyshire spar, backed with clunch raised at Burwell, about eleven miles from Ely. It has wings or side screens all of clunch; from the base-moulding the walls are covered with a diaper flower carved in alto-relievo, exhibiting a series of lilies, apparently connected together by their stems, running through the frames in which each flower rests; above, on each side, is an arcading consisting of three open arches having geometrical foliated tracery, topped with a cornice of many mouldings, with a slope above surmounted by a cresting of flame-like form.

"The front of the central portion on each side of the Altar above the base-moulding is covered with diaper carved in alto-relievo, exhibiting a series of roses, apparently connected by the stems, running through the pattern; above these and the Altar it is divided into five compartments, four of which are occupied by two trefoils each, and the centre by three trefoils, sunk by a hollow moulding which is gilt, and ornamented with Ball-flowers and filled in with mosaic work of verde antico, rosso antico, and lapis lazuli; over these are five panels cut in alabaster, containing alto-relievo sculpture of considerable merit; commencing on the north side, the first is Christ's Entry into Jerusalem; second, Christ washing his Disciples' Feet; third, The Last Supper; fourth, Christ's agony in the Garden, and lastly, Christ bearing his Cross. In the front, and at the division of each panel, stand three spiral columns, the sunk Screen having a gold ground, on which are set cornelian and agate stones alternately. The spiral columns have rich foliated capitals; at the division are larger supporting figures of angels bearing the Nails, the Hammer, the Crown of Thorns, the Spear, the Cross, instruments of Our Lord's Passion; on each side of the principal shafts, and in the centre of each panel, is a smaller but similar column, supporting two gabled canopies, over each sculptured panel, springing from a dragon or grotesque figure, and finished with a finial; the inner portion of each gable contains within a circle a head in basso-relievo; those on the north side, of the prophets Isaiah, Jeremiah, Ezekiel, and Daniel; those on the south, the four doctors of the Church, St. Jerome, St. Ambrose, St. Augustine, and St. Gregory. The other portions, as well as the panels of the shafts of the finials, are filled in with rich and costly mosaics. The centre compartment has three projecting gabled canopies, the sunk gables and panels of which are filled with mosaics. Above the centre on a lofty, enriched pinnacle is a figure of our Lord. On the north side, on a lower pinnacle, is a figure of Moses, and on the other side a figure of Elias. The upper portion of the Screen is set back carved in clunch — except the figure, which is in alabaster — and divided into five compartments of openwork, surmounted by a rich cresting. In front rise five gables, the centre being larger and higher than the others, with a figure of our Lord enthroned on the apex. It is filled in with a trefoil, containing a basso-relievo of the Annunciation in alabaster and made up with mosaics. The foliated crocketing of the gable contains the pelican feeding her young. The four side gables each support a figure of one of the four Evangelists, their respective emblems being worked on the crockets. In the inner faces of the gable, within the trefoils, are busts in basso-relievo, those on the north side representing St. Mary Magdalene and St. Mary the Mother of Jesus, those on the south side, St. John the Baptist and St. John the Divine. The spaces in the gables are filled in with mosaics. Outside and between these gables rise spiral columns supporting alabaster figures of the virtues, Faith, Hope, and Charity; on the north side those of the graces, Justice, Prudence, and Fortitude.

"Sir George Gilbert Scott was the architect, but the Dean and Mr. Gardner took great interest in the work, and suggested some of the important features in it, such as the mosaics, sculpture, decorations, etc. The whole of the stonework, including the architectural carving but not the sculpture, was executed by Mr. Rattee, the sculp-

ALTAR AND REREDOS IN ELY CATHEDRAL

ture by Mr. J. Phillips, the mosaics by Mr. Field, and the decoration by Mr. Hudson, of Kensington Museum. The latter was a work of much labor, requiring great knowledge and experience. The gentle touch of gold and the mingling colors produce a most pleasing effect. The friezes of the robes are most exquisite, and the diapers are very skillful performances. On a work so profuse it was most difficult to know where to leave off. Even now one sees so much of the charming and beautiful for his mind to feed upon, that the separation creates a lingering feeling not to leave such a treasure. The Reredos itself, as already stated, was the magnificent gift of John Dunn Gardner. Dean Peacock gave £200 for the side screens, and the remainder was defrayed by the Dean and Chapter. It was commenced in 1850, but was not completed until 1868." One in authority reports the entire cost as something over £4000.

THE CATHEDRAL CHURCH OF ST. MARY, SALISBURY

THE Altar is built of English oak. The design is that of an arcade with seven openings, divided into three panels with elaborate carvings. The Altar was given by those persons who had received confirmation through Bishop Hamilton. The Reredos is designed from the old choir Screen in the Lady Chapel of the Cathedral. The central panel, eight feet high, has in relief the Crucifixion, with the Virgin Mary and St. John. At the top of the central arch are angels and foliage. The canopied niches on the sides of the Crucifixion contain figures of the two Marys, and of St. Osmund and Bishop Beauchamp. The whole structure terminates in a gemmed and floriated cross. The Reredos was designed by Sir George Gilbert Scott and executed by Farmer and Brindley. It was the gift of Earl Beauchamp in memory of Bishop Beauchamp. The cost was over £1800.

ALTAR AND REREDOS IN SALISBURY CATHEDRAL

ALTAR AND REREDOS IN EXETER CATHEDRAL

THE CATHEDRAL CHURCH OF ST. PETER, EXETER

The Reredos was erected in 1876, and is constructed of marble and alabaster. It rises thirty feet from the floor, and was designed by Sir George Gilbert Scott. It was the gift of Chancellor Harrington and Dr. Blackall. The canopies are of verde antico marbles, and the whole structure is surmounted by a floriated cross. There are three sculptured compartments. The central one represents the Ascension, the one on the right the descent of the Holy Ghost at Pentecost, and the one on the left the Transfiguration. The whole is profusely inlaid and gemmed. Among the jewels are the amethyst, cornelian, jasper, onyx, malachite, garnet, bloodstone, and lapis lazuli. The Retable is of polished alabaster and marble mosaics. The Altar-cloth is of crimson velvet and is rich in needlework of silk and gold and is resplendent with jewels, pearls, and crystal drops. This also was designed by Sir George Gilbert Scott. The Altar and Reredos cost something over £2000.

THE CATHEDRAL CHURCH OF ST. PETER, GLOUCESTER

The Reredos was unveiled in 1873 with special services. It was the gift of the Treasurer of the Province. It was designed by Sir George Gilbert Scott. The groups of figures were sculptured by Redfern. The central compartment represents the Ascension of our Lord. On either side may be seen the Nativity and Burial of Christ. In the four separate niches are Moses, David, St. Peter, and St. Paul. In the upper turrets or niches are nine angels bearing emblems of the Passion. The Reredos has recently been extensively gilded. Its cost was £1500.

ALTAR AND REREDOS IN GLOUCESTER CATHEDRAL

By permission of Valentine and Sons, Dundee.
ALTAR AND REREDOS IN ROCHESTER CATHEDRAL

THE CATHEDRAL CHURCH OF ST. ANDREW, ROCHESTER

The old Altar, dating from 1707, was a plain structure constructed of Norway oak. Above this was hung in 1788 a picture of "The Angels appearing to the Shepherds," by Sir Benjamin West. In 1826 this picture came into the possession of St. Mary's Church, Chatham. In 1873 the Restoration Committee added the present Altar and Reredos, from designs by Sir George Gilbert Scott. The Altar is a solid oak structure, and the Reredos is built of Caen stone. A representation of the Last Supper is sculptured upon it. Some of the later improvements in the general effect of the Altar and Reredos have been made by the present architect of the Cathedral, Mr. Hodgson Fowler.

THE CATHEDRAL OF ST. PETER, YORK

The Triptych was erected in 1878, and is constructed of oak and terra-cotta, painted and gilded. The central compartment contains a representation of the Crucifixion in relief. Mr. G. E. Street was the architect and Mr. Tinworth the builder. The Triptych is a memorial to Mrs. Markham.

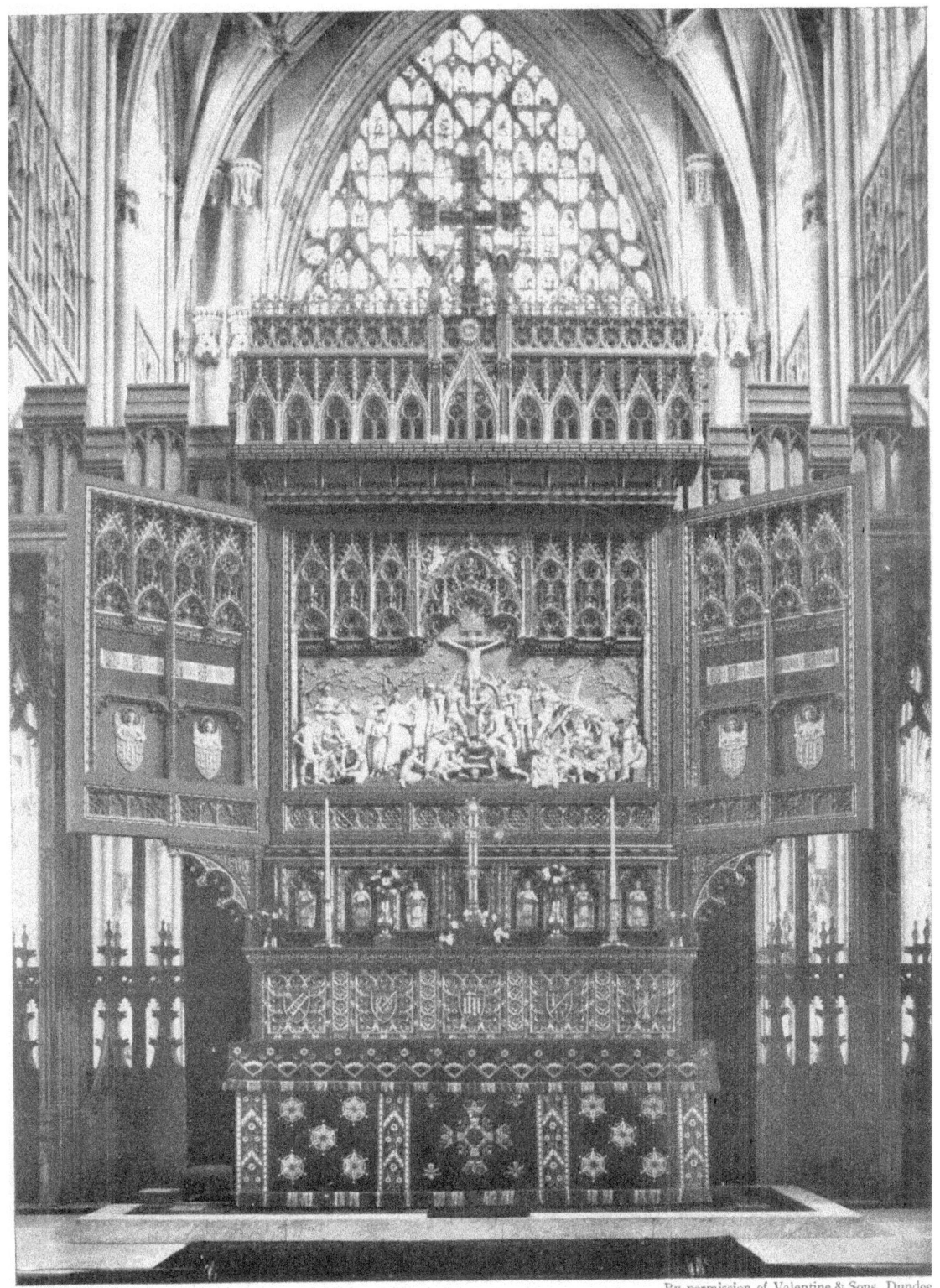

By permission of Valentine & Sons, Dundee

ALTAR AND TRIPTYCH IN YORK CATHEDRAL

ALTAR AND REREDOS IN WORCESTER CATHEDRAL

THE CATHEDRAL CHURCH OF CHRIST AND THE BLESSED MARY THE VIRGIN, WORCESTER

The Reredos is constructed of alabaster enriched with malachite, agate, lapis lazuli, and other colored stones and marbles. It was designed by Sir George Gilbert Scott and erected by Farmer and Brindley. In the central niche is the seated figure of Christ in the act of benediction. In the canopied niches on each side are the figures of the Four Evangelists. A great cross surmounts the whole. The Reredos was given to the Cathedral by Dean Peel, a brother of the eminent statesman of that name. On an inlaid cross is the following inscription: "In memory of John Peel, D.D., Dean of this Cathedral from A.D. 1846 to 1874, who erected this Reredos in affectionate remembrance of Augusta his wife; this cross is inscribed by the Dean and Canons and other friends A.D. 1877." The cost of the Reredos was £1500.

THE CATHEDRAL CHURCH OF ST. MARY, TRURO

"STANDING below the Sanctuary steps, which are of lovely Italian marble, delicately veined, we look up at the magnificent Reredos of richly carved Bath stone. The general idea of the sculpture is 'the one great sacrifice of our Blessed Lord,' made with bloodshedding on the cross, represented in the 'Crucifixion,' immediately above the Altar, and as pleaded continually in heaven, represented in the 'Majesty' which fills the upper part of the central portion of the Reredos; while on either side are typical subjects of the older Covenant, representing the great foreshadowing of Sacrifice for sin, of the gift of Life, of Communion with God, and of self-oblation.

"Examining the Reredos in detail, it will be observed that the whole is designed in three great sections, a central and two side ones; each subdivided into separate portions by tiers of recessed and richly canopied niches, the composition forming, with its splendid groups of sculptured figures, not only a work of beautiful symbolic art, but a most effective instrument of devotional and sacramental teaching.

"In the central section our attention is first of all directed to the offering of the great High Priest of the 'one oblation of himself once offered on the Cross.' The sculptor has succeeded in combining that which it is so difficult to do, the true pathos of human suffering with the dignity of the Divine Personality of the holy victim.

"All the details of the great and awful event are treated historically and yet devotionally. On either side of the crucified Son of God are the Blessed Virgin Mary and St. John; at the foot of the cross Mary Magdalene embraces the sacred feet; the other Mary offers consolation to the sorrowful mother. The purpose of the Saviour's passion includes Jew and Gentile, and so are seen in the group Hebrew Rabbis, the Roman Centurion with his soldiers, and a man of the people holding a lantern; that the event is one that concerns not earth only but the unseen world is shown by the presence of ministering angels, whose ninefold choirs are also indicated in the nine small niches immediately above the Altar, and in the adoring representatives of the

ALTAR AND REREDOS IN TRURO CATHEDRAL.

heavenly hosts in the eight pairs of niches on each side of the central section. Below these angelic figures on either side, close to the Altar, are the figures of the four Evangelists, in the pages of whose writings are recorded with such emphatic fullness all the details of the Saviour's Cross and Passion and Resurrection.

"Then above, in the upper division of the Central Section, we see the figure of the same Jesus, 'Who, for the joy that was set before Him, endured the cross, despised the shame, and is now set on the right hand of the Majesty on high.' There is the great High 'Priest upon His Throne,' crowned and robed, holding the Book of Life, 'ever living to make intercession,' 'appearing before God for us,' surrounded by angels and amidst the glory of the 'Redeemed from among men,' lifting his Hands in blessing upon his Church as at the Ascension.

"Then on either side are the great historical preludes of this mighty mystery.

"1. Righteous Abel and his sacrifice of faith looking forward to the sprinkling of that Blood 'which speaketh better things' than that of the first witness slain for God's truth.

"2. Noah, who walked with God and offered his oblation of thanksgiving for redemption from the punishment that overtook the ungodly.

"3. The Tree of Life — the Sacrament of Life in Paradise — emblem of the living Sacrament of life in the Church on earth, and of the bliss of eternal communion in heaven.

"4. The Sacrifice of Isaac — faint type of the gift of an eternal Father, 'Who spared not his own Son.'

"5. The Brazen Serpent — type of the uplifting of the Son of Man on the Cross to redeem mankind from the curse of sin.

"6. Feasting on the Paschal Lamb — the figure of him that was to be 'the very Paschal Lamb, that taketh away the sin of the world,' and Whose Flesh is 'meat indeed' for his people.

"7. The Shew Bread — the emblem and the memorial of the self-oblation and the consecration of the twelve tribes, and of mystic communion with God in his Sanctuary, to be realized in a far deeper sense and meaning in the Eucharistic feast, where Christians feed on the Bread of Life, and 'offer themselves, their souls and bodies, as a living sacrifice' to God, their reconciled Father.

"8. The gathering of the first fruits — fulfilled in the Resurrection of the Son of God, 'the first fruits of them that slept' in the Sanctification of the Church as 'a kind of first fruits of His creatures,' and in the consecration to God in this present world now, and hereafter at the great harvest, of all the best gifts of spirit, soul, and body that man possesses, redeemed and made 'fit for the Master's use.'

"In the outer tiers of niches are seen the figures of the prophets who spoke beforehand of all this: Isaiah, the Evangelical prophet; and Daniel, the prophet of Messiah's Kingdom; Amos, the shepherd prophet of the Church's glory; Zechariah, the prophet of the priesthood; Jeremiah, the prophet of mercy and judgment; Joel, the prophet of penitence; Malachi, who foretold the oblation of the pure offering of the Eucharist. And then the Apostles and Martyred Saints of the Christian Church. The twelve great 'Foundations' of the Church grouped in the lower subdivisions of the two side sections, and in the tiers of niches representatives of later Martyrs of varied rank and station and time;

"St. Edmund, the English Christian King, shot to death by heathen Danes. St. Cecilia, the sweet singer and Virgin Martyr. St. George, the Saintly Soldier Martyr of Cappadocia, Patron of England. St. Vincent, the martyred Deacon of Spain, who, with St. Lawrence, bore witness with his blood in the great persecution under Diocletian. St. Catherine, the cultured Virgin Martyr, patroness of philosophy and learning. St. Polycarp, the holy Bishop and Martyr of Smyrna. St. Lawrence, the Holy Archdeacon of Rome and Martyr. St. Alban, Proto-Martyr of Britain."

"This magnificent Reredos is the gift of the Deanery of Powder, and is the work of Mr. N. Hitch, of Kensington. This work of art was erected in 1887, and the architect was Mr. J. L. Pearson, R.A."

The above description was furnished in printed form through the courtesy of Canon Gardiner, of Truro.

ALTAR AND REREDOS IN LICHFIELD CATHEDRAL.

By permission of Valentine & Sons, Dundee.

THE CATHEDRAL CHURCH OF ST. CHAD AND ST. MARY, LICHFIELD

The Reredos was erected in 1855, and is constructed of alabaster with inlaid marbles. An effort was made to have all the material come from the Diocese. This was done, with the exception of the malachite. The alabaster came from Tutbury and the rich red marble from the quarry of the Duke of Devonshire. The Reredos is divided into five compartments, with richly decorated pediments, the central one being larger and more elaborate than the others. Above it rises a highly carved pinnacle surmounted with a cross. In this central compartment is a representation of the Ascension. The panels on each side contain the emblems of the four Evangelists. The Reredos was designed by Sir George Gilbert Scott, and cost £2000. This sum was raised by Mrs. H. Howard, the wife of the Dean.

At a later day an improvement was made by the addition of the arcading on either side of the Reredos. This was filled with twelve statues of alabaster about three feet and six inches high. On the north side, beginning at the Reredos, are St. Andrew, St. Ignatius, St. Nicomede, St. Stephen, St. Alphege, and St. Perpetua. On the south are St. Paul, St. Polycarp, St. Lucian, St. Lawrence, St. Alban, and St. Blandinia. This addition was designed by Mr. C. E. Kempe and executed by Farmer and Brindley. The cost was £600.

THE CATHEDRAL CHURCH OF ST. MARY, ST. GEORGE, AND ST. DENYS, MANCHESTER

The Reredos was given in 1894 by the family of the late John Allen. It is of carved wooden work and extensively painted and gilded. It is constructed with seven vertical sections and two lateral divisions, the latter being in two tiers. The three niches in the centre contain figures of St. Mary, St. George, and St. Denys. The latter two were added as patron saints under Henry V, who was King of England and of France. Above all in a canopied niche is a seated figure of Christ holding in one hand an orb and a cross, while the other is raised in benediction. The smaller panels are made to illustrate the words of the Sanctus, "With angels and archangels," etc. The Reredos was erected from designs by Mr. Basil Champneys.

By permission of William H. Bowman, Manchester.

ALTAR AND REREDOS IN MANCHESTER CATHEDRAL

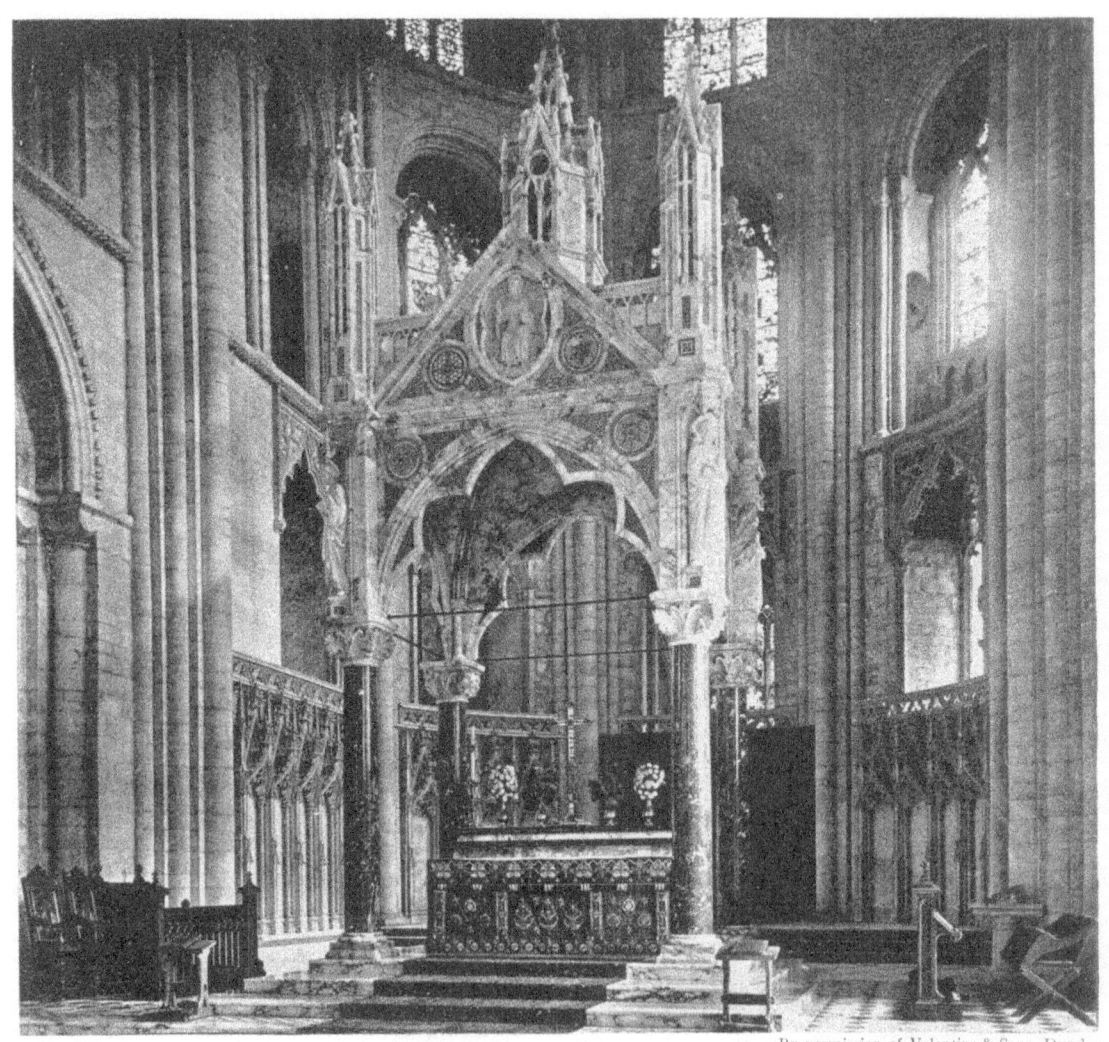

ALTAR AND BALDACHINO IN PETERBOROUGH CATHEDRAL

THE CATHEDRAL CHURCH OF ST. PETER, PETERBOROUGH

The Altar and Baldachino are erected upon a dais thirteen feet square, and the distance to the top of the central spire is thirty-five feet. Four marble columns stand at the corners, supporting niches in which are placed figures of the Evangelists. The arches and spandrels are generously enriched with mosaics. The central panel has in front a figure of our Lord and in the back one of St. Peter. The material used is Derbyshire alabaster. The Altar and Baldachino were erected by the eight children of Dean Saunders as a memorial of their father and mother. The Retable was the gift of certain graduates of the King's School. The builder was Mr. Robert Davison, of London.

THE CATHEDRAL CHURCH OF ST. MARY AND ST. ETHELBERT, HEREFORD

The Reredos was erected in 1850, of Bath stone and marble. It was designed by Mr. Cottingham, Jr. There are five deep panels arranged under canopies. The panels are divided by small shafts, supporting angels who carry the symbols of the Passion. The subjects executed by the sculptor, Mr. Boulton, are as follows: The Agony in the Garden, Christ Bearing the Cross, The Crucifixion, The Resurrection, and The Three Women at the Sepulchre. The Reredos is a memorial to Mr. Joseph Bailey, who served several years in Parliament. The upper part of the arch over the Reredos is occupied by a spandrel which is covered with sculpture representing our Lord in Majesty, surrounded by the four Evangelists holding scrolls. Below this is a statue of King Ethelbert.

By permission of Valentine & Sons, Dundee.

ALTAR AND REREDOS IN HEREFORD CATHEDRAL

ALTAR AND SCREEN IN THE CATHEDRAL OF ST. ALBAN

THE CATHEDRAL CHURCH OF ST. ALBAN

The great Screen dates from the fifteenth century. It was built by Abbot William Walyngforde, and was one of the chief glories of the Abbey before violent hands were laid upon it. So complete was the destruction that it is impossible to say what were its original ornamentations. Of the statues, only the fragments of two remain, the one of the feet and drapery of a figure supposed to be a Bishop, and the other the lower portion of the form of St. Stephen clad in a dalmatic. But happily through the offerings of the generous, and the consecration of artistic minds, the Screen has been restored in part at least to its original beauty. Lord Aldenham devoted himself to the work and restored the canopies and filled them again with statues. The making of the statues was intrusted to Mr. Harry Hems, of Exeter, the larger one being constructed of limestone from Mansfield Woodhouse, Nottinghamshire, and the smaller ones of alabaster. The Screen proper is built of a hard stone quarried at Tottenhoe, near Dunstable, and is in dimensions forty-two feet high by thirty-nine feet wide, reaching from the north to the south side of the Sanctuary. It is divided perpendicularly into three sections. The central one is a representation of the Crucifixion, with three niches on each side and the two wings. It was also divided laterally. Both on the eastern and western faces of the Screen are numerous large and small niches. The whole is intended to represent the Passion of our Blessed Lord. On the side of his cross stand St. Mary and St. John. On either side of these are angels, and four angelic attendants are also arranged on the sides of the head of Christ. Below the central group are thirteen colored niches and canopies containing our Lord seated in majesty with six apostles on either side. Below this is a representation of the Body of our Blessed Lord after it had been taken down from the cross. It is attended by the Blessed Virgin and the other two Marys. Soldiers and other figures appear in the background. This special work was executed by Mr. Alfred Gilbert.

On the Epistle side of the Altar, arranged in the larger and smaller niches, are St. Amphibalus, the English martyr; St. Patrick, the Apostle of Ireland; St. Hugh, Bishop of Lincoln; St. Alphege, Archbishop and martyr; St. Osyth, the founder of a monastery; St. Wulfstan, Bishop of Worcester; St. Lucy, Virgin and Martyr; St. Lawrence, Deacon and Martyr; Edward, King of the West Saxons; St. Etheldreda, the Abbess of Whitby; Adrian IV, Bishop of Rome; St. Ælfric, Abbot of St. Albans and Archbishop of Canterbury; St. Margaret, of Scotland; St. Richard, Bishop of Chichester; St. Ethelburga, Abbess of the Monastery of Barking; St. Benedict, Bishop, Abbot of the Monastery of St. Peter and St. Paul at Canterbury and founder of the Monasteries at Wearmouth and Jarrow; St. George, the patron saint of England; St. Erkenwald, Bishop of London; St. Germain, Bishop of Auxerre; and the Venerable Bede, the father of English learning.

On the Gospel side are arranged St. Alban, the protomartyr of Britain; St. Benedict, the founder of the Benedictine monastic order; St. Edward the Confessor; St. Chad, Bishop of York; St. Frideswide, the Abbess of a monastery; St. Nicholas, Bishop of Myra in Lycia; St. Agnes, Virgin and Martyr; St. Leonard, Deacon; St. Ethelbert, King and Martyr; St. Helena, the mother of Constantine; Offa, King of Mercia; St. David, Archbishop of Menevia; St. Katherine, of Alexandria; St. Boniface, Bishop of Mainz; St. Cecilia, Virgin and Martyr; St. Giles, Abbot; St. Oswin, King of Deira; St. Augustine, Archbishop of Canterbury; St. Cuthbert, Bishop of Lindisfarne; and St. Edmund, King and Martyr. Lord Aldenham, in speaking of the way he was guided in the selection of statues, says: "My purpose in the choice of the personages whom they were to represent, has been to select English saints, or saints especially connected with England, and particularly those who had any relation with St. Albans; and when no such qualification existed, I have selected for the remaining niches saints who had Altars in the Abbey, or who were commemorated in our own kalendar. Among the greater statues I have included two other personages who were not canonized, but whom the citizens of St. Albans should particularly hold in honor. These are Offa the Second, King of Mercia, and Nicholas Breakspear, otherwise called Adrian the Fourth, the only English Pope."

This description has been condensed from the admirable "Account of the High Altar Screen in the Cathedral Church of St. Albans" by Lord Aldenham.

ALTAR AND REREDOS IN THE CATHEDRAL OF ST. NICHOLAS, NEWCASTLE–ON–TYNE

THE CATHEDRAL CHURCH OF CHRIST AND THE BLESSED VIRGIN MARY, CHESTER

THE Altar and Reredos were erected in 1876, the architect being Sir George Gilbert Scott. Farmer and Brindley executed the work. The Altar is made of wood given by Mrs. Lee, who brought it from the Holy Land, cedar, olive, and fig wood. The Reredos has a representation of the Last Supper done in mosaics by Salviati, of Venice. Its cost was £1200, and the Altar an additional expenditure of about £100.

THE CATHEDRAL CHURCH OF THE HOLY TRINITY, BRISTOL

The Reredos in Bristol Cathedral is not only an artistic and stately structure, but it is rich in its historic suggestions. It not only contains figures of Prophets and Apostles, but many names identified with early British Christianity. They are arranged in the following order:—

1. St. Augustine, of Hippo, founder of the rule of monastic life followed to a great extent by the Austin Canons of St. Victor, who served the Abbey.
2. St. Augustine, of Canterbury, who met the British Bishops not far from Bristol.
3. Birinus, first Bishop of the West Saxons.
4. St. Chad, Bishop of Mercia.
5. St. Aldhelm, Abbot of Malmesbury and first Bishop of Sherborne.
6. St. Hilda, Abbess of Whitby, to mark the Northumbrian origin of Bristol Christianity.
7. Bosel, first Bishop of Worcester (resigned in 691).
8. St. Wulfstan, Bishop of Worcester, who by preaching and influence suppressed the slave trade at Bristol.
9. Robert Fitzhardinge, founder of St. Augustine's Abbey, Provost of Bristol and Canon of St. Augustine's.
10. St. Thomas, of Canterbury, who was Chancellor, issued the first Charter of Liberties to the burgesses of Bristol, in 1155, and whose name stands first among the witnesses to the charter.
11. John Wycliffe, Prebendary at Aust, in the Collegiate Church of Westbury-on-Trym.
12. William Canynges, five times mayor of Bristol and Dean of the Collegiate Church of Westbury-on-Trym.
13. Hugh Latimer, Bishop of Worcester.
14. Sir Jonathan Trelawney, Bishop of Bristol, who was sent to the Tower in June, 1688.
15. Joseph Butler, Bishop of Bristol.
16. Charles John Ellicott, Bishop of Worcester and Bristol.

The architect was J. L. Pearson, and Fitch Vauchet, sculptor. The cost was about £2500.

ALTAR AND REREDOS IN BRISTOL CATHEDRAL, BRISTOL

ALTAR AND REREDOS IN CHRIST CHURCH CATHEDRAL, OXFORD

By permission of Henry W. Taunt & Co., Oxford.

THE CATHEDRAL CHURCH OF CHRIST, OXFORD

THE Reredos was erected in 1881, and is constructed of red Dumfries sandstone. It was designed by Mr. Bodley. The central panel represents the Crucifixion, with the Virgin Mary and St. John at the foot of the cross. In the distance is a view of Jerusalem. St. Michael, clad in armor, and St. Stephen, in a dalmatic, are in the niches in the left. In the niches on the right are St. Augustine in cope and mitre, and St. Gabriel. The six shields above the niches contain the emblems of the Passion. The small angel on the left of the Crucifixion bears a chalice, and the one on the right, the crown of thorns. The figures were sculptured by Mr. Brindley. The High Altar is built of cedar-wood, and the eight legs are covered with gilded carvings. In 1901 parts of the Reredos were decorated in color and gilding.

THE CATHEDRAL CHURCH OF ST. CUTHBERT AND ST. MARY, DURHAM

The Screen is only a remnant of what it once was, and simply a suggestion of its former glory, when all its niches were resplendent with statues. It is known as the "Neville Screen," because it was erected about the year 1380, chiefly through the liberality of John, Lord Neville, of Raby. Another has said, "Though very light and graceful in appearance, the Screen as it is at present can give the beholder little idea of what its appearance must have been when each of its canopied niches contained a figure aglow with gold color. There were originally one hundred and seven of these statues, the centre one representing Our Lady, supported on either side by St. Cuthbert and St. Oswald." Even in its denuded condition it has an artistic effect at once stately and majestic.

ALTAR AND PARTIALLY RESTORED SCREEN IN DURHAM CATHEDRAL

ALTAR AND PARTIALLY RESTORED SCREEN IN CHICHESTER CATHEDRAL

By permission of W. H. Barrett, Chichester.

THE CATHEDRAL CHURCH OF THE HOLY TRINITY, CHICHESTER

An ancient Screen supposed to have been erected by Bishop Sherburne, in 1508, did service for many years in the Cathedral. In the course of time it became dilapidated, and was removed in 1860. In its place a marble and alabaster Reredos was erected, having in the central portion a representation of the Ascension. It was not regarded as altogether satisfactory, as it seemed to be out of keeping with its surroundings. In 1904 it was given to the Church of St. Saviour, Preston, Brighton, and it was determined to restore the ancient Screen. The design for the restoration was drawn by Mr. Somers Clarke, and the work executed by Norman and Burt, of Burgess Hill. The Screen is a fine example of oak carving. Much of the old oak in the paneling and the canopies has been retained. At some future date the design will be completed by the addition of a carved representation of the Crucifixion and figures of the Apostles. An inscription cut in the back reads, "Giving glory to God, and in grateful and affectionate remembrance of Francis John Mount, Archdeacon of Chichester, his many friends reërected and restored this ancient screen, 1904." The unveiling service took place on January 12, 1905, when there was a representative gathering of the Cathedral and local clergy, with many friends of the deceased Archdeacon. The dedicatory prayers were offered by the Dean, and the unveiling by the Bishop of the Diocese, who formally handed the Screen over to the custody of the Dean and Chapter.

THE CATHEDRAL CHURCH OF ST. NICHOLAS, NEWCASTLE-ON-TYNE

The Reredos was erected in 1887. The late R. J. Johnson, of Newcastle, was the architect. The carver of the structure was R. S. Beall. The sculptor of the alabaster figures was Mr. James Sherwood Westmacott, of London, brother of Mr. Percy Westmacott, of Newcastle, the donor of the Reredos. The perpendicular style that prevailed in the fourteenth century was followed. Directly above the Altar in the small niches are nine angels holding shields with emblems of the Passion. Above these, and arranged on each side of the central canopies, are ten figures representing the same number of virtues. These are as follows: —

Faith, holding a cross; Hope, holding an anchor; Charity, ministering to two children; Justice, with scales and a sword; Temperance, with a bridle; Chastity, with a dove and a sceptre; Humility, bearing a yoke from our Lord's own words, "Take my yoke upon you"; Prudence, holding a serpent, from "Wise as serpents, and harmless as doves"; Fortitude, with a stout staff; and Patience, with a ball in her hand and her foot upon a crown. The rest of the description can be best told in the words of the architect. He writes: "The great central niche above has the enthroned figure of our Lord, one hand raised in benediction, the other supporting an orb with a cross on it. On either side are the figures of the four Evangelists, with their emblems, and beyond these are those of St. Gabriel and the Blessed Virgin, one on each side. Below these two are the figures of St. Wilfrid and St. Paulinus. The upper row begins, on the left, looking eastward, with St. Oswald, next to whom comes the Venerable Bede. Then we have St. Nicholas, the patron saint of the Church. The central place is given to St. Cuthbert, the most famous of the Northumbrian saints, who carries the head of St. Oswald. Then comes St. Aiden, Cuthbert's predecessor, St. Benedict Biscop, the founder of the monasteries of Wearmouth and Jarrow, and lastly, St. Edwin the King. The material used is finely selected English alabaster, the figures being purely white and

By permission of F. & W. Dodsworth, Newcastle-on-Tyne.

ALTAR AND REREDOS IN THE CATHEDRAL OF ST. NICHOLAS, NEWCASTLE-ON-TYNE

the structure graduated in color, the work nearer the floor being darker, and the whole carefully chosen of paler tint towards the upper part. A rich cornice and brattishing finish the top of the Reredos, with a spire over the central canopy that contains the figure of St. Cuthbert. Splayed screens of Caen stone, paneled and traceried, connect the Reredos with the pillars of the arcade on either side, and westward come the sedilia on the south, with corresponding recesses on the north side, all worked out in Caen stone, with very rich canopy-work pinnacles and brattishing."[1] The cost of the Reredos was £4000.

[1] *The Reredos in Newcastle Cathedral*, pp. 12, 13.

THE CATHEDRAL CHURCH OF ST. PAUL, LONDON

The Sanctuary of this Cathedral is a noble and commanding example of ecclesiastical art. The Screens and Reredos were designed by those widely known English architects, Bodley and Garner. The latter gentleman read the following account before the St. Paul's Ecclesiological Society: —

"The design consists of a basement, against which the Altar stands, with small doorways, to give access to the apse behind. Over these doorways, which are of pierced brass, are angels supporting the crossed swords and keys, the arms of the diocese, and emblems of St. Paul and St. Peter, and they are flanked by sculptured festoons of fruit and flowers separated by marble panels. Above this is a range of sculptured panels with colored marble backgrounds, supporting an open colonnade of semicircular plan. A large group of sculpture, a sort of carved picture in bold relief, occupies the centre, flanked on each side by twisted columns of rich Brescia marble, wreathed with foliage in gilded bronze. These support an entablature and rich pediment. The frieze is of rosso antico, bearing the inscription '*Sic Deus dilexit mundum*' ('So God loved the world') in gilt-bronze letters. The whole is crowned with a central niche and surrounding statues, at a height of between sixty and seventy feet from the ground.

"The general idea of the sculptured subjects is to express the Incarnation and Life of our Lord, beginning with the two figures at the extremities of the colonnade, which are those of the angel Gabriel and St. Mary, and represent the Annunciation. The panel on the north side is the Nativity; the large subject in the centre the Crucifixion, with the Entombment beneath it; and the group on the south side the Resurrection. The panels of the pedestals are filled with angels bearing instruments of the Passion. The niche above the pediment is occupied by the figure of St. Mary, with the Divine Child in her arms, with the statues of St. Paul and St. Peter on either hand. The figure on the summit of the niche is an ideal one of the risen Saviour.

"The entire Altar Screen is executed in white Parian marble, with bands and panels of rosso antico, verde di Prato, and Brescia marbles.

ALTAR AND REREDOS IN ST. PAUL'S CATHEDRAL, LONDON

The enrichments are generally gilt, the steps in front of the Altar are of white marble, and the pavement of rosso antico, Brescia, verde di Prato, like the Reredos."

The Reredos rises to a height of seventy-five feet. It cost the sum of £28,000, and the Screens £5500. The Altar was the gift of Mrs. Ambrose, the sister of the late Rev. Dr. Liddon.

THE CATHEDRAL CHURCH OF ST. SAVIOUR, SOUTHWARK, LONDON

THE Altar Screen has much historic interest. It dates from 1520 and is ascribed to the generosity of Bishop Fox, who a little before had bestowed a like gift upon Winchester Cathedral. The Rev. Canon Thompson, M.A., D.D., the present Rector and Chancellor of the Cathedral Church of St. Saviour, writes: " The Screen, which is about thirty feet in height, is divided horizontally, as in the Winchester example, into three stages or stories. Vertically it is also tripartite. This arrangement was adopted in allusion to the sacred number three. The most important variations from its original design, for which Wallace, the architect, who restored it in 1833, is responsible, consist in the addition of the cornices, filled with angels, above the lowest and second stories, and over the third, the range of angels holding shields. But the most significant change was the introduction of niches, in the middle space of the lowest stage, behind the High Altar. This space, which seems to have been an exact square, was left entirely blank by Fox, with the exception of two small niches, one on each side, close to the ogee-headed doorways. The Winchester Screen possessed this same peculiarity. The blank was evidently intended by the Bishop to be occupied by some work of art in painting, sculpture, or mosaic. And when we proceed to fill the niches with statues, a work which will no doubt be soon taken in hand, it would be only fair to the memory of the munificent Prelate, who has left us this valuable legacy, to return to his original design. The corresponding space in Winchester Cathedral, which for some years had been occupied by Benjamin West's picture of the Raising of Lazarus, is now filled with niches containing figures of some minor saints. At present our Screen is like a picture frame without the picture — a scene of magnificent emptiness. But when the niches are filled up with appropriate statues, what a resplendent spectacle we shall have in this Choir — an assemblage of angels and saintly men of the past, prophets and apostles uniting, as it were, in the glorious anthem *Te*

By permission of Canon Thompson.

ALTAR AND PARTIALLY RESTORED SCREEN IN SOUTHWARK CATHEDRAL

THE CATHEDRAL CHURCH OF ST. SAVIOUR

Deum Laudamus. The ancient materials of the Screen consist of Caen and firestone. Painswick stone was used in its restoration. Such portions as are new were scrupulously worked from models made from the original remains, and replaced in the same situations which were occupied by the originals." He also adds: " Considerable portions of the original remain. The background or foundation of the Screen is old. When the wooden Baldachino was removed, the large central niche in the uppermost tier possessed remains of an elegant canopy enriched on the under side with elaborate fan-tracery; the five smaller niches on either side of it contained similar interesting details. The angular buttresses springing from the ground and separating them appeared to have been untouched, and these were preserved where possible. The cornice surmounting the whole was enriched with the Agnus Dei and the Pelican, interspersed with oak leaves and acorns, and in the pedestals were figures of angels and lions, grotesque heads and foliage. In the cornice of the middle stage two monks, holding a shield between them, formed the prevailing device, the intervening spaces being filled with roses, lilies, and twisted thorns, showing also the head of the Saviour, and that of St. John, beautifully moulded, all in the highest state of preservation, and as fresh as if they had just come from the sculptor's hands. In the lowest stage the doorways were discovered uninjured and also the niches, canopies, and pedestals, with carvings and enrichments similar to those already described."[1]

[1] *The History and Antiquities of the Collegiate Church of St. Saviour*, pp. 317, 318, 319.

WESTMINSTER ABBEY, LONDON

The Altar and Reredos were erected in 1867 after a design by Sir George Gilbert Scott. The central compartment is done in mosaic by Salviati and represents the Last Supper. The sculptured figures are by Mr. Armstead.

In *The Globe* of September 1, 1866, appeared the following: "A beautiful and valuable mosaic picture on gold ground representing the 'Last Supper' has just been completed for the Dean and Chapter of Westminster, and will shortly be placed in the Reredos of the Abbey. Dr. Salviati, although he has only for a few years turned his attention to the production of mosaic works, has attained considerable celebrity in the art, and by the production of a pure and durable enamel, his mosaics are considered to equal, and even surpass, those of the ancient masters."

ALTAR AND REREDOS IN WESTMINSTER ABBEY

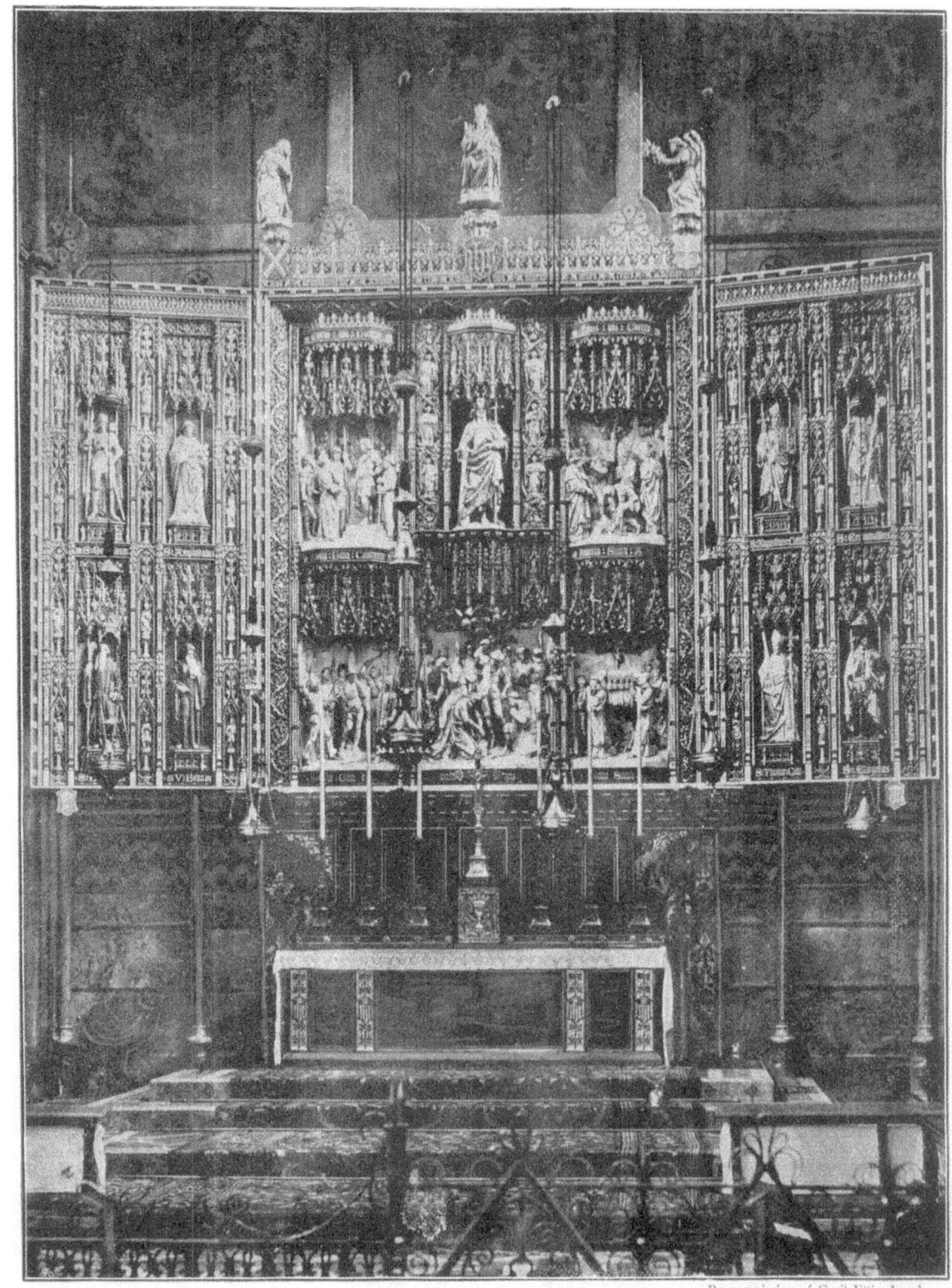

By permission of Cyril Ellis, London.

ALTAR AND TRIPTYCH IN THE CHURCH OF ST. ALBAN THE MARTYR, HOLBORN, LONDON

THE CHURCH OF ST. ALBAN THE MARTYR, HIGH HOLBORN, LONDON

A BOOK published in the interests of the parish contains the following description of the High Altar: —

"The great central piece is divided into six compartments, arranged in the following way: —

"The Trial, St. Alban, The Finding of his Relics, The Scourging, The Martyrdom, The Translation to St. Alban's Abbey.

"The left wing (spectator's left) contains the following large figures: —

"St. George, St. Benedict, St. Amphibalus, Ven. Bede, and twelve smaller figures.

"The right wing contains the following large figures: —

"St. Augustine of Canterbury, St. Thomas of Canterbury, St. Erconwald of London, St. Edward, King, and twelve smaller figures.

"The inscription running along the top of the central piece is 'Ave prothomartyr Anglorum, miles Regis Angelorum. Albane, flos Martyrum' ('Hail! Proto-martyr of the English, Soldier of the King of Angels. O Alban, flower of martyrs'). The words are from the Antiphon on his Feast Day.

"The three detached figures which rise above the rich cresting are, in the centre, the Lord seated upon His throne, His hand raised in blessing, Our Blessed Lady, and the Archangel Gabriel.

"The subjects of the centre-piece are carved in alabaster set in a massive frame of oak. The important lines and features of the sculpture are touched with gold; the lining of the draperies painted a pale and quiet blue. All the woodwork, with its richly moulded canopies, buttresses, pinnacles, etc., is gilt upon red, but the gold is everywhere lacquered in varied tones of green and brown and red. The sculptures of the wings are all in wood, gilt, and colored. The massive hinges which connect them with the centre are relieved of some of the weight by wrought-iron brackets, which support the outer corners of the wings. These ponderous masses of knotted oak swing quite easily when, in Passiontide, the doors are closed.

"The whole was designed by Messrs. Bodley and Garner, and executed by Messrs. Farmer and Brindley."

ST. PAUL'S CHURCH, KNIGHTSBRIDGE, LONDON

The Reredos was erected in 1870 of stone. The central compartment has the Crucifixion with historic characters on either side. The large figures are St. Ambrose, St. Augustine, St. Jerome, and St. Gregory. The architect was R. H. Withers. The building of the Reredos around the east window is a somewhat novel treatment.

ALTAR AND REREDOS IN ST. PAUL'S CHURCH, KNIGHTSBRIDGE, LONDON

By permission of Cyril Ellis, London.

ALTAR AND REREDOS IN ST. STEPHEN'S CHURCH, LONDON

ST. STEPHEN'S CHURCH, KENSINGTON, LONDON

The Reredos is arranged in three tiers. The figures are of carved wood, richly gilded, with a background of red. In the centre of the first tier is a representation of our Lord in glory, in the attitude of blessing. Angels are on either side. These figures are nearly life size. In the second tier the figures are smaller. The Nativity is in the middle and the Annunciation on either side. In the third tier the Blessed Virgin is in the centre. On the left are Moses, Isaiah, and St. John the Baptist. On the right are St. Stephen, St. Peter, and St. Paul. The figures were carved by Mr. Bridgeman, of Lichfield, and decorated by Mr. Powell, of London. The contractor was Mr. Martin, of London, and the architect Mr. Bodley. The cost was about £500. The Reredos was erected in 1901.

CHURCH OF THE HOLY REDEEMER, CLERKENWELL, LONDON

The Baldachino was begun in 1888 and completed in 1895. It is constructed of brick, cement, and wood, with pillars, friezes, etc., in Scagliola, and surface with ornamental work in plaster. It was designed by J. D. Sedding, the architect of the church, after a work of a similar character in marble and bronze over the High Altar of San Spirito in Florence. The work was begun by Pomeroy and Cay, and finished by Rider. It cost something above £600.

ALTAR AND BALDACHINO IN THE CHURCH OF THE HOLY REDEEMER, CLERKENWELL, LONDON

By permission of Cyril Ellis, London.

ALTAR AND REREDOS IN THE CHURCH OF ST. JOHN THE DIVINE, KENSINGTON, LONDON

CHURCH OF ST. JOHN THE DIVINE, KENSINGTON, LONDON

THE Altar is of cedar-wood and was erected in 1874.

" The Reredos reaches almost to the groining of the roof. It is of wood, beautifully carved by Messrs. Farmer and Brindley, the well-known art sculptors of Westminster Bridge Road, and occupies the whole space of the easternmost span of the apse. The frame is of most elaborately carved work, painted red, and almost entirely covered with gold. All round the frame there runs a most delicate cresting, which gives considerable lightness to what is in itself a very massive structure, and the carving of the inner frame represents grapes and corn. Immediately above the Altar there are three shelves, on the front of the middle of which is written : —

"' Benedictus Qui venit in Nomine Domini.'
"' Blessed is He that cometh in the Name of the Lord.'

" The Reredos is divided into two main divisions, in each of which there is a large central subject flanked by a figure on either side. In the lower compartment we have represented to us the Annunciation. The Blessed Virgin is kneeling on a faldstool, inscribed with the word ' Emmanuel,' and dressed in the traditional blue robe, whilst the Angel Gabriel in a white robe, and with golden wings and lily in his hand, is announcing to her the high honor to which she is called. Beneath, in gilt letters, is the angelic salutation: ' Ave Gratia Plena.' On the south side of the Annunciation is the figure of St. Hugh, Bishop of Lincoln, in which diocese this part of the country used to be, represented with his traditional swan, and on the north side St. Augustine of Canterbury, as one to whom we owe so much for the revival of the Catholic religion in this fair land of ours. In the upper compartment there is, as the central subject, the Crucifixion, with St. Mary and St. John at the Cross, and on either side, above St. Hugh, the figure of St. Michael, clad in armor, and St. Raphael above St. Augustine of Canterbury, exhibiting him in the dress of a pilgrim or traveller : ' his habit fit for speed succinct': sandals on his feet, his hair bound with a diadem, the staff in his hand, and a bottle of water slung over his shoulders. Above all there is a pinnacled coving — red and gold — with the legend: —

"'Sic Deus dilexit mundum,'
"'So God loved the world,'

written thereon." The above account is taken from a parish publication. The Reredos was designed by Sir G. F. Bodley and cost £700.

ALTAR AND REREDOS IN THE CHURCH OF ST. MARY, SOHO, LONDON

ST. MARY'S CHURCH, SOHO, LONDON

The Altar is of oak, designed by an architect who was a pupil of Mr. Street. It was built at a cost of £150. It is in dimensions ten feet long, twenty-nine inches broad, and thirty-nine inches high. On the front of the Altar are four angels bearing shields. On the shield of the first appear a chalice and paten, on the second a lamb and flag, on the third a pelican, and on the fourth a serpent on a cross. There are also three panels containing deeply cut representations of the Annunciation, the Adoration of the Magi, and the Presentation in the Temple. The figures have been recently decorated by gilding. The large crucifix is of marble and was sculptured by Miss Grant of Chelsea. St. Mary's Church has a very unique history.

The Nave was the first Greek Church in England; built by the Archbishop of Samos for Greek exiles in 1677; used afterwards by the Huguenots for one hundred and forty years, till 1832; introduced by William Hogarth into his picture, "Noon," 1738; occupied by Calvinist Pædo-Baptists until 1849; consecrated for the Church of England, 1850; became a parish church in 1856; described by Hall Caine in *The Christian;* destroyed by the London Common Council as a "dangerous structure" in 1898; and rebuilt, and reopened in April, 1901. Corner-stone of chancel was laid by Canon Liddon, in 1872.

CHURCH OF ST. AGNES, KENSINGTON, LONDON

The Triptych or Altar-piece is a memorial erected in 1891 by the then Vicar of the parish, the Rev. T. D. Dover, in memory of his mother. It is made of oak elaborately decorated in gold and colors. In the centre is a sculptured group representing the Annunciation. About it are figures of the twelve apostles, St. Agnes, St. Cuthbert, the Venerable Bede, St. Ethelbert, St. Columba, St. Augustine, and others. The architect was Sir George Gilbert Scott. Mr. Temple L. Moore largely assisted in the details and in the general superintendence of the work. The designs were executed by Mr. Elwell and the sculptured figures by Farmer and Brindley. The cost was about £600.

ALTAR AND TRIPTYCH IN THE CHURCH OF ST. AGNES, KENSINGTON, LONDON

ALTAR AND REREDOS IN ST. BARNABAS CHURCH, PIMLICO, LONDON

ST. BARNABAS CHURCH, PIMLICO, LONDON

The Reredos was erected in 1892, and throughout is constructed of wood. In the middle of the lower line of figures we have the Annunciation, and on the right hand St. Barnabas and St. Anselm of Canterbury. On the left hand St. Paul and St. Augustine of Hippo. The middle of the second line is occupied with the Crucifixion, the Blessed Virgin, and St. John. On either side are two angels. Mr. Bodley was the architect, and the figures were carved in Belgium. The cost of the whole was £1000.

ST. JOHN'S CHURCH, HACKNEY, LONDON

In the *St. John at Hackney Magazine*, for September, 1904, the history of the Reredos, written by one of the Curates and sent by the courtesy of the Vicar, the Rev. Algernon G. Lawley, M.A., reads thus:

"The following inscription is written on a brass band at the base of the carving, 'Dedicated to the Glory of God A.D. 1886, by the Rector of the Parish and his wife in thankful memory of their father, John Jackson, Bishop of this Diocese 1869–1885.' The Rector at that time was the Rev. Arthur Brook, whose wife was a daughter of Bishop Jackson.

"The architect was Sir Arthur Blomfield, and the sculptor Mr. Forsyth of Finchley Road, N.W.

"The Reredos is carved in bold relief in oak, the total cost being some £350.

"The general idea is that of witness to Christ, and the five panels illustrate the texts of Scripture above which they are placed. The large central panel is a picture of St. John i. 34: 'And I saw and bare record that this is the Son of God.' The scene is laid on the banks of the Jordan. In the lower part St. John the Baptist, clothed in his camel-skin, stands out boldly from among his disciples and with uplifted arm is pointing to the central figure of our Lord. A second text is carved below, 'Behold the Lamb of God which taketh away the sins of the world.'

"On either side are two smaller panels, and the same idea of witness is still the dominating note. In the upper panels St. John is delivering his message and preparing the way, whilst in the lower panels the Holy Ghost is descending and taking up the work and sending men forth with strength and power to carry on the life of witness among their fellow-men.

"On the left-hand or dexter side the two texts illustrated are: first the prophecy, 'He shall baptize with the Holy Ghost,' and the fulfilment, 'They were all filled with the Holy Ghost.' Above we have St. John baptizing in the Jordan, and the crowd standing watching on

ALTAR AND REREDOS IN ST. JOHN'S CHURCH, HACKNEY, LONDON

the bank recalls the story of St. Luke who tells us of the people and the publicans and the soldiers who came to ask what the prophet would have them do. Below we see the outpouring of the Holy Ghost on the great day of Pentecost and the tongues of fire descending upon the waiting Apostles.

"On the other side the two texts are: 'He must increase, but I must decrease,' and 'The Holy Ghost came on them.'

"The idea would seem to be expressed by the word of the prophet, 'Not by might, nor by power, but my spirit, saith the Lord of Hosts.' Reliance must be placed, not on man, but upon the Holy Spirit of God working within us. Above the first text there stands St. John preaching to the people, at once the boldest and the humblest of obedient messengers. Below we have a picture of an early Confirmation, the simple laying-on-of-hands by an Apostle upon two young men, kneeling to receive God's gift of the Holy Spirit, that they may do the work whereunto God has called them."

CHURCH OF ST. GILES, CRIPPLEGATE, LONDON

The Reredos is modern and was erected about twelve years ago. The middle painting represents Christ as the King of Kings and Lord of Lords. On the Epistle side is a figure of St. Paul and on the Gospel side one of St. Giles. All the three paintings were executed by Mr. C. E. Buckeridge. The carvings of angel heads, the eagle, the vine and grapes are effective and artistic.

ALTAR AND REREDOS IN CHURCH OF ST. GILES, CRIPPLEGATE, LONDON

By permission of Cyril Ellis, London.

ALTAR AND REREDOS IN OLD ST. PANCRAS CHURCH, LONDON

OLD ST. PANCRAS CHURCH, LONDON

THE present Vicar, the Rev. Robert A. Eden, writes: "At old St. Pancras Church, London, we are still in possession of the old Altar stone which has come down to us apparently from Norman times. In 1848 the tower at the west end of the Church was pulled down to lengthen the nave. At that time the Altar stone was discovered, buried about six feet below the surface of the ground. It must have been placed there in Reformation times, either, if the Vicar of that day was a man of Catholic views, to save it from desecration at the hands of the destroyer, or else, if he was of Puritan sentiments, to prevent such a 'monument of superstition' from ever again seeing the light. However that may be, the stone was, on its discovery, placed under the Altar, where it formed part of the Sanctuary pavement. It was there, at any rate, safe from desecration and could not be trodden upon, as the Altar stood over it. In 1888 the Chancel was rearranged, and at that time the present Altar was constructed in the following way. The front and the two ends were made of the fine-carved and inlaid oak panels of a seventeenth-century oak pulpit, which then stood in the Church, but which had to be removed. Three panels were in front and one at each end. A new oak mensa was made, and the old Altar stone was inserted in the midst of it, so that its surface was flush with the surface of the rest of the mensa. The Altar stone is quite small, being about seventeen inches long and nine inches wide. When the new Altar was made, orders were given that every part of the table which had served as the Altar in recent times, say for two hundred years, should be employed in the backing or some other part of the new structure; so our present Altar may be said to be three Altars formed into one. The size of the present Altar is thirty-eight inches high, twenty-six inches wide, and seven feet long. The Reredos consists of a carved oak triptych, with mahogany panels richly colored and gilded. It was made in 1897 by Thompson of Peterborough from a design by the late Sir A. W. Blomfield, A.R.A. The painting and gilding are the work of Messrs. Buckeridge and Floyce, artists of great promise, who both died in very early life. On the central panel is represented our Lord upon the Cross, with St. Mary on the one side and St. John on the other. On the lower panel of the left wing or folding door of the triptych is St. Pancras, the boy-martyr, holding in his left hand a book, and in his right a sword and a palm branch, the one the instrument and the other the symbol of his martyrdom, while he tramples upon a fallen idol, an action indicating the moral effect of his faithfulness unto death. On the opposite wing appears St. Paul, the Patron Saint of the Cathedral of the Diocese. He is introduced to mark the connection between the Cathedral and Old St. Pancras Church, the vicarage of the latter having been in the gift of the Dean and Chapter of St. Paul's from about the year 1100. The four panels over the two patron saints contain the apocalyptic emblems of the four Evangelists. The Triptych rests upon the upper shelf of a Retable of black marble; the lower, a broader shelf of the same material, is some ten or twelve inches above the Altar, and supports the Altar cross and candlesticks. The back of the folding doors, which are kept closed in Lent, is simply treated with a powdering of conventional flowers in gilt upon a dull red ground."

ALTAR AND TRIPTYCH IN THE CHURCH OF ST. MARY THE VIRGIN, PRIMROSE HILL, LONDON

CHURCH OF ST. MARY THE VIRGIN, PRIMROSE HILL, LONDON

THE Triptych was designed by Sir G. F. Bodley at a cost of £700. The material is wood painted red with gilding. In the centre are the Virgin and Child with an angel on either side. In the same row are Isaiah and St. John the Baptist. The Annunciation is below. The Altar is nine feet one inch long, two feet eight inches wide, and three feet three inches high. The mensa rests on an arcade of wood. There are four iron posts, with copper sconces for candles by Harold Staller. The cost of the Altar was £20. The dorsal, the frontal of tapestry, and frontlet of velvet are the work of the St. Dunstan Society. The cost was £19. The Vicar of this parish is the Rev. Percy Dearmer, M.A., widely known as the author of *The Parson's Handbook*. The Altar of the parish is arranged according to the directions of this book.

CHURCH OF ST. ANNE, EASTBOURNE

The central subject of the Altar Screen is our Lord, as the Saviour of the world, attended by six adoring angels.

On either side are figures of St. William of York and St. George of England. St. William was chosen in reference to the name of one of the persons commemorated in the memorial, St. George as the saint of the country.

In the remaining and outside niches of the Altar Screen are figures of the angel Gabriel and the blessed Virgin Mary, representing the Annunciation.

Beneath is a row of angels with shields. These figures are of stone in full relief, painted and gilt.

In the middle panel of the Reredos proper are two seated figures, with space for the Altar cross between them. These are, on one side, St. Anne, to whom the Church is dedicated; on the other side, our blessed Lord as a child, in the arms of his mother St. Mary, to whom the mother Church of the old parish is dedicated. These figures were chosen, therefore, in allusion to the two parishes.

In the two next panels are figures of St. Anne with St. Mary as a child, in further allusion to the dedication of the said parishes; and St. Elizabeth with St. John Baptist as a child, St. Elizabeth being chosen in reference to the name of the other person commemorated by the memorial.

The same references are to be found in the remaining figures of St. Anne and St. Joachim, and St. Elizabeth and St. Mary in the Visitation in the two end panels of the Reredos.

Between each of these panels is a small angel with uplifted wings in full relief.

The figures on the panels are, on the contrary, in low relief, and gilt all over, upon a gilt background broken by a small colored diaper. The whole of the Reredos proper is of pine. W. Bucknall and J. N. Comper were the architects. The cost was about £600.

ALTAR AND REREDOS IN THE CHURCH OF ST. ANNE, EASTBOURNE

By permission of Cyril Ellis, London.

ALTAR AND REREDOS IN ST. MARY'S CHURCH, CUDDINGTON

ST. MARY'S CHURCH, CUDDINGTON

The Altar is of oak and was in an earlier Church that stood on this spot. The Reredos was unveiled on Whitsunday, 1902. It is built of Carrara marble with alabaster supports. The compartment in the centre represents Christ blessing little children. St. Peter, St. James, and St. John are on the Lord's right hand, a group of parents and children on his left, and a child on his knee and others at his side, The Reredos was given by Mr. C. W. Wismith in memory of his wife. At the time he was the church warden. The architect was J. A. Thomas, and the builders, Farmer and Brindley. The walls of the apse are beautifully finished with polished stones.

CHURCH OF ST. CUTHBERT, NEWCASTLE-ON-TYNE

The whole apse of this Church is rich in its incentives to the Christian life as represented in its art creations. The Reredos is an epitome of the leading scenes from the life of our Lord as narrated in the New Testament. Towering above all is the Crucifixion, and in the central panel below this is the Transfiguration and still lower the Last Supper. On each panel on either side of the Transfiguration are the Baptism of Christ and his Temptation. On the side panels of the Last Supper are Christ washing the feet of the disciples and the woman annointing our Lord. On the south door of the Reredos are representations of Christ presented in the temple and the Adoration of the Magi. On the back of this door, not seen from the front, are Christ before Herod and our Lord bearing his cross. On the north door are the Annunciation and the Nativity. On the back of the door are Christ in the Garden and Pilate washing his hands. On the lower and smaller south door is a representation of Christ driving out the traders from the Temple, and on the back of the door the Betrayal by Judas. On the lower north door is the scene of Christ entering Jerusalem on an ass, and on the back of the door St. Peter's denial of his Master. The decoration of the walls of the apse on each side of the Reredos is a paneling in mahogany and lime-tree divided by the words, " The Holy Church throughout the world doth acknowledge Thee, the Father of an infinite Majesty; Thine honorable, true and only Son; the Holy Ghost, the Comforter." In the upper portion are sixteen paintings. Those on the Epistle side are Abraham, Moses, Aaron, David, Isaiah, St. John the Baptist, the Blessed Virgin Mary, and St. Peter. On the Gospel side the paintings represent St. Paul, St. Stephen, St. Alban, St. Ambrose, St. Hilda, St. Cuthbert, St. Gregory the Great, and St. Anselm.

The wood carving, which is exceedingly decorative and effective, was designed by Mr. Ralph Hedley. The Reredos was the result of designs by Hicks and Charlewood, the paintings in the Reredos by Burlison and Grylls, and the sixteen paintings on the sanctuary walls by Bacon Brothers.

For much of this description of the Reredos of St. Cuthbert's Church we have drawn from the account written by the Rev. W. E. Nowell, D.D., the first Vicar of the parish.

ALTAR AND REREDOS IN THE CHURCH OF ST. CUTHBERT, NEWCASTLE-ON-TYNE

ALTAR AND REREDOS IN THE CHAPEL OF MARLBOROUGH COLLEGE

CHAPEL OF MARLBOROUGH COLLEGE, MARLBOROUGH

THE Altar and Reredos are built of Corsham stone, colored. In the central compartment is a representation of the Crucifixion with St. John and St. Mary. Above this the Adoration of the Magi. The topmost pinnacle contains a figure of the Saviour. The eight figures on each side are: 1. Angel with staff. 2. Archangel with trumpet. 3. Angel of principalities. 4. Angel of powers. 5. Angel of virtues. 6. Angel of dominations. 7. Angel of thorns. 8. Cherub singing.

CHAPEL OF JESUS COLLEGE, OXFORD

THE Altar is a granite slab resting on six pillars of the same material. The Reredos dates from 1864. There are three panels of marble. The central one represents the Crucifixion with a group of four figures at the foot of the cross. The panel on the right indicates Christ bearing his cross, and the one on the left has our Lord supported on the knees of St. Mary. The Reredos was erected at the time of the restoration of the Chapel by Mr. Street. The builder was Mr. Wyatt of Oxford. The whole cost of the restoration was about £1500.

ALTAR AND REREDOS IN CHAPEL OF JESUS COLLEGE, OXFORD

ALTAR AND SCREEN IN THE CHAPEL OF ALL SOULS' COLLEGE, OXFORD

CHAPEL OF ALL SOULS' COLLEGE, OXFORD

The Reredos dates from the foundation of the College about the year 1438. The chapel and its adornments were greatly mutilated during the Reformation by the Puritans. A wall of mortar was built across the rear of the Altar, completely covering up the canopied figures. Streeter, the court painter of Charles II, painted a fresco of the Last Judgment on this wall. It was not pleasing to all, for Evelyn thought it "too full of nakeds, for a chapel." About 1770 this fresco was replaced by one by Sir J. Thornhill representing the apotheosis of Archbishop Chichele, the founder of the College. Mr. C. Grant Robertson writes: "The Chapel, in short, took the form it was to wear for two centuries, and it is almost pathetic to observe how effectually these changes obliterated the memory of its original appearance. All Souls' literally forgot that it once had a Reredos and a hammer beam roof, and De Wenman, writing at the end of the eighteenth century, does not, for all his erudition, betray the faintest glimmer of a suspicion as to what lay behind the lath and the plaster of 1665."[1] In 1872 the fifteenth-century roof came to light and then the sculptured treasures behind the plastered wall. In 1878-79 the Chapel was completely restored at an expense of over £10,000. Mr. Robertson, in speaking of the original condition of things, says, "The High Altar was adorned with the image of the Holy Trinity gilt and painted, and in the space over the Altar was placed a representation of the Crucifixion, while at the summit of the Reredos immediately under the roof was the figure of our Lord seated in judgment surrounded by archangels and marked with the inscription, 'Surgite mortui, venite ad Judicium.'"[2] The structure is built of Bath freestone. At the restoration the sculptor Geflowski introduced the features of some of the modern Fellows of the College. Thus on the right of the crucifix, between Archbishop Warham and Bishop Goldwell, he has depicted Lord Salisbury as John of Gaunt.

[1] *All Souls' College*, pp. 139, 140. [2] *Ibid.*, pp. 14, 15.

CHAPEL OF MAGDALEN COLLEGE, OXFORD

The Rev. Frank E. Brightman, M.A., a Fellow of Magdalen, writes:—

"The arrangement of the Screen behind the Altar which is the same type as that of New College and All Souls' is probably on the lines of the original Screen of about 1475, which was defaced in 1549. The present restoration was made in 1829 to 1834, except in regard to the statues, which were not added until 1884, though they were included in the architect L. N. Cottingham's plans of 1829. The statues in the niches are all Old Testament personages with the exception of one, that of St. John the Baptist. In the centre of the top story is the 'Noli me tangere.' The picture over the Altar is our Lord bearing the Cross, by Ribalta. It was taken from a Spanish ship at Vigo in 1702, brought to England by the Duke of Ormond, and presented to the College in 1745, by one W. Freman, an undergraduate of the College in 1719. It was placed in the centre of the present Screen in 1758, and so remained until the restoration, when it was set in the stone work that now surrounds it. The Altar is of stone and is part of the restoration of 1829."

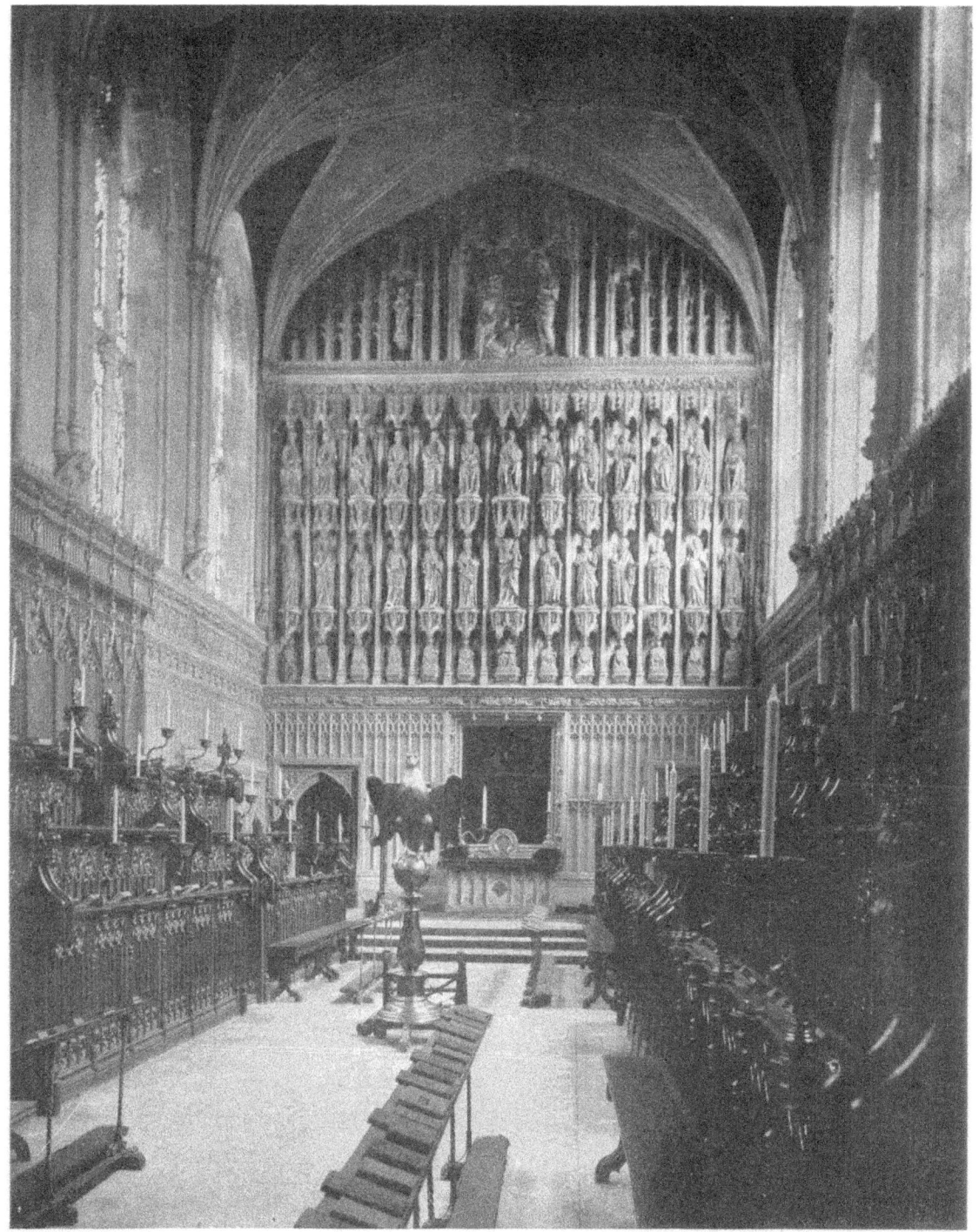
ALTAR AND SCREEN IN THE CHAPEL OF MAGDALEN COLLEGE, OXFORD

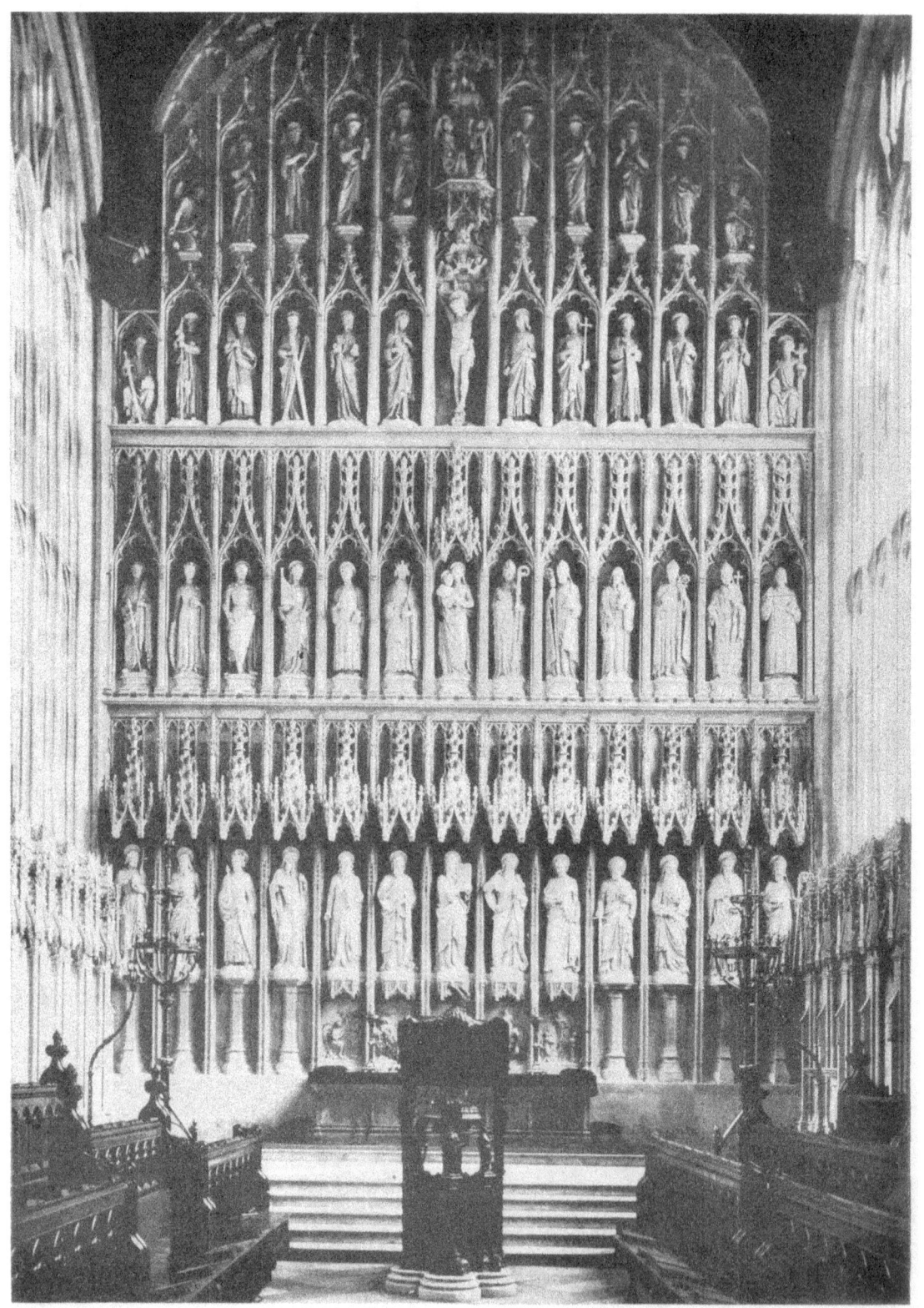

ALTAR AND SCREEN IN THE CHAPEL OF NEW COLLEGE, OXFORD

CHAPEL OF NEW COLLEGE, OXFORD

THE Screen represents generally the Orders enumerated in the Te Deum. In the highest row we have the Agnus Dei accompanied by Angels. In the second row a representation of the Crucifixion has six Apostles on the right and left. The third row has the Virgin and Child in the centre with King Richard II, St. Stephen, St. Cecilia, St. George, St. Catherine, and St. Alban on the north side, and William of Wykeham, St. Augustine, Bede, St. Anselm, Warham, and Ken on the south side. The fourth row contains Moses holding the Tables of the Law, with the four greater prophets, Isaiah, Jeremiah, Ezekiel, and Daniel in the centre and Samuel, David, Elijah, and St. John the Baptist on the north side and St. Paul, St. Jerome, St. Chrysostom, and St. Ambrose on the south side. The design of the niches is supposed to be of William of Wykeham's time, that is of 1379. The statues that stood in them were removed and broken up in the reign of Edward VI, and the niches were filled up in accordance with an injunction of Robert Horn, Bishop of Winchester in 1567. Later in 1789 the Reredos was restored in plaster. The niches were replaced in stone in 1879 under Sir George Gilbert Scott, and the statues were restored in 1890–92 under Mr. J. Pearson. The contractors for the work were Farmer and Brindley of London, and N. Hitch, an English workman, executed the statues. The entire restoration was made possible through the gifts of members of the College.

CHAPEL OF WINCHESTER COLLEGE

The original stone Reredos dates from the building of the College from 1387 to 1393. In later years its suffered from changes and mutilations. There are still traces of original painting, but not enough to form a design or pattern. Sir W. Earl restored the Reredos in 1866. The figures, also of stone, were erected in 1876, by the Master of the College. The statues represent St. Peter, St. John, St. James, St. Stephen, St. Paul, St. Augustine, William of Wykeham, Alfred the Great, and others. There is no record of the first cost of the Reredos, or of its restoration, but the stone figures were erected at an expense of £25 each.

ALTAR AND REREDOS IN THE CHAPEL OF WINCHESTER COLLEGE.

By permission of H. W. Salmon, Winchester.

ALTAR AND REREDOS IN ST. JOHN'S COLLEGE, HURSTPIERPONT

By permission of St. John's College.

ST. JOHN'S COLLEGE, HURSTPIERPONT

THE story of the building of the Altar and Reredos is admirably told in the *Hurst Johnian Magazine*. After speaking of the starting of a special fund in 1865, this publication proceeds to say:—

"Seven years passed, and Christmas, 1872, saw the work finished, a tribute to the honor of God, the beauty of which is hardly to be matched in England. With the exception of the centre sculpture, given by one since gone to his rest, all this was done by no large subscriptions, but by the patient ingathering of small sums, gifts, and thank-offerings, savings, profits, and earnings, in wonderful variety. The secret of success was the determination to go on with the work step by step, as money was forthcoming. The Rev. Lewin Pennell gave the crowning ornament of all, — 'a Pelican in her piety,' the ancient emblem of him whose Body was torn, and whose Blood was poured out on the Cross for his people.

"The four figures below were added in memory of the Rev. John Gorham, by the many friends who mourned his loss in 1866, and thus, gradually, memories and associations came to add interest to the work. Bishop Gilbert was moved to tears, as he ministered at the Altar, by the pathetic beauty of the Virgin Mother's sculptured form, standing by the Cross of Jesus. John Keble helped with advice and money. William Campion of Danny and many other friends since fallen asleep lent their aid. The three chief groups of sculpture represent the 'Agony in the Garden,' the 'Crucifixion,' and the 'Burial of our Lord.' The base of these three sculptures is raised one foot nine inches above the top of the Super-Altar; the height and width of the central one are respectively ten feet and seven feet; and of the side compartments, nine feet and five feet six inches. The figures are a little under life size.

"Each of the three groups of sculpture stands in an arched and canopied recess, the arches being supported on piers of stone and clustered marble columns, and flanked by lofty pinnacles. The space below the central sculpture is of course filled by the Altar, but underneath the compartments on either side are four arched and canopied niches, and the side pinnacles are continued downward as columns to the footpace, on which the Altar stands. Immediately above the Super-Altar, and below the base of the sculpture, runs a richly moulded cornice of varied alabaster, ornamented with semi-balls of sienna, Irish green jasper, and Blue John spar. On this rests the base of the piers, supporting the columns and pinnacles. These piers consist of a centre of moulded Caen stone, in front of which are four detached columns, supporting the canopies and pinnacle above, and on each side are two pillars, from the capitals of which spring the arches of the great canopies over the sculptures. These columns are of Cat Down spar, Galway-green marble, and alabaster; they have moulded bases of alabaster, and are tied together by annulets, also of alabaster. The capitals are of Caen stone, carved and ornamented with bosses of red and green marble, with alabaster neckings. The height from the cornice above the Altar to the top of the caps is five feet six inches, the total height from the floor to the top of the centre finial being twenty feet. The main arch over the central group of sculpture rises above five feet, and is of richly moulded Caen stone; and below it is a subordinate trefoil cusped arch, also of moulded stone. The circles and spandrels between these two arches are filled in with marble mosaics. In the circles are the Alpha and Omega, in white alabaster, on a ground of emperor's red marble; and the mosaics in the spandrels are in patterns of contrasted marbles on a dark green ground.

"The triangular spandrels above the great main arch, and the pediment mouldings, are inlaid with a ground of varied and polished alabaster; immediately above the point of the circle is a quatrefoil-shaped panel of moulded Caen stone, inlaid with agate. Touching the four points of the quatrefoil is a moulded cross of pure white alabaster, one foot high, the centre being formed by a faceted circle of green marble; the spaces between the arms of the Cross and the mouldings of the quatrefoil are filled with bosses of Pyrenean jasper on a green marble ground. The great spandrel is also ornamented with inlays and bosses of sienna, green marbles, and Blue John spar.

"The mouldings of the pediment are of Caen stone; on the upper side are richly carved crockets and bases, on which stand the four

Evangelists, two on either side. On the south side, St. Matthew and St. Mark, and on the north side, St. John and St. Luke. The mouldings terminate at the top in a carved and moulded finial, resting on which is the pelican shedding its blood to feed its young. Supported on the capitals of the previously described four detached and projecting columns, are the bases of the niches, and the pinnacles above. The canopies of the niches are formed by moulded arches, resting on columns of Brocatella marble, with bases and caps of Caen stone. There are three figures in each of these four niches; the twelve figures being probably as follows, commencing at the north side: St. Jude, St. Philip, St. Matthias, St. Thomas, St. Peter, St. Barnabas, St. James, St. Paul, St. Andrew, St. Bartholomew, St. Simon, St. James the Less. St. Matthew and St. John are omitted, as occupying a place in their character of Evangelists. These figures are about one foot eight inches high.

"The moulded pediments of the niche canopies are ornamented with carved crockets and finials, into which are introduced bosses of green marble and alabaster. The spandrels above the arches are filled with marble mosaics on an alabaster ground. Resting on these canopies is the cylindrical base of the pinnacle, on which are eight columns of jasper, sienna, green, and red marbles, surrounding a stone centre, with carved caps, supporting a moulded and carved cornice, ornamented with bosses of sienna marble. The top of the pinnacle is circular, and inlaid with bends and patterns of dark alabaster, and terminates in a richly carved stone finial. As before mentioned, there are on each side of the Altar, below the great side groups of sculpture, four recessed niches; these are formed by moulded and cusped arches of alabaster, supported on shafts of colored marbles, with bases and capitals of alabaster. These bases rest on a moulded plinth of red Mansfield stone, which also forms the plinth of the whole composition. The arches of the niches are surmounted by crocketed pediments of alabaster, the finials and crockets of which are ornamented with bosses of marble. The spandrels of the arches are filled with marble mosaics. The alabaster moulded cornice over the altar is continued, and is intersected, by these pediments. The projecting flank pinnacles are supported on shafts of polished granite, with alabaster caps and bases. In these niches stand Caen stone figures of the eight Doctors of the Eastern and Western Church. The first on the north side is St. Gregory, W., St. Basil, E., St. Jerome, W., St. Athanasius, E. The first on the south side, next the Altar, comes St. Ambrose, W., St. Chrysostom, E., St. Augustine, W., and St. Gregory Nazianzen, E. These have all been special gifts, and have cost sixteen guineas each. The centre sculpture contains nine large figures, besides two smaller figures of angels. Our Saviour hangs dead on the Cross, his arms wide stretched, his head bowed towards the right, on which side is a group of the Holy Women; Salome, mother of St. John, and St. Mary, the wife of Cleophas, supporting the almost fainting form of the blessed Virgin, and St. Mary Magdalene kneeling in loving humility, embracing the feet of Christ; beside her, that alabaster box of ointment wherewith she 'did what she could.' On the other side is the Centurion, who was the first to make confession of the Godhead of the Crucified, also kneeling; and behind him stand St. Joseph of Arimathæa, Nicodemus, and St. John, the beloved disciple.

"The sculpture on the north side represents the Agony; St. John sleeps in the foreground, his head resting on his hand; whilst further back our Saviour kneels, as in that mysterious hour of woe, one angel reverently supporting Him, and others of the Heavenly hosts looking on, with folded hands, in wonder. Beneath a great stone a serpent lies crushed — emblem of him who first, in a garden, won victory, and again, in a garden, was bruised and vanquished by a Stronger than he.

"The sculpture on the south side represents the Entombment, in which St. John, and St. Joseph of Arimathæa, and another, tenderly lay the dead Body of our Lord in the Tomb, while the women stand or kneel in various attitudes of grief.

"All these sculptures were executed by Mr. Forsyth, of London; the canopies by Messrs. Poole, of London, and Allen, of Leicester. The whole has cost about £2000.

"The Super-Altar is white Carrara marble, and has stones inlaid in various designs; the stones include agate, jasper, cornelian, crystal, malachite, amber, pink coral, bloodstone, etc."

ALTAR AND REREDOS IN THE CHAPEL OF CHELTENHAM COLLEGE

By permission of Cheltenham College.

CHAPEL OF CHELTENHAM COLLEGE

"In Memory of old Cheltonians who fell in the South African War of 1899–1902" is the inscription upon the Cheltenham Reredos. This is indicative of the patriotic spirit that stimulated the erection of this artistic production. The Reredos has been rightly described as "a great work, a worthy memorial, an inspiring history in stone." The architect and builders are residents of Cheltenham; the former Mr. H. A. Prothero, and the latter R. L. Boulton and Sons. The material used is clunch from Cambridgeshire. The cost reached £1459.

The central compartment represents Christ on the cross, not in agony, but with a face full of tenderness and hope as he looks out over a world he has redeemed. On either side of his head is an adoring angel and below are St. Mary and St. John. The large figures about the cross in niches represent prominent characters associated with the history of England. On the Gospel side in the upper row are Becket and Langton. In the lower niches are Dunstan and Anselm. On the Epistle side in the upper niches are Bede and Cranmer, and in the lower Wycliffe and Tyndale. Below the cross in a small grouping is the Adoration of the Magi, and on one side are the archangels, Michael, Gabriel, Raphael, and Uriel, and on the other side are the saints, David, Patrick, Andrew, and George. Returning to the larger statues, those on the upper row, on the Epistle side, are Wesley, Rakes, and Howard, and those in the lower niches, Keble, Colet, and Wilberforce. The symbols below the pedestals represent Fortitude, Truth, and Justice. The three large statues on the Gospel side are St. Alban, King Arthur, and King Edmund, and below are Columba, Augustine, and Aidan. The symbols below the feet are Faith, Hope, and Charity. The large figures are each four feet high, and appear in the costume of their time. The small figures, two feet high, are arranged in the four buttresses. Beginning on the left we have in art and science Chantrey, Reynolds, Wren, Handel, Claxton, and Newton. In the second buttress, administration, education, and leadership are indicated by Lawrence, Simon of Montfort, Arnold, Wykeham, Gordon, and King Alfred. In the third buttress, representative of literature, learning, and leisure, are Shakespeare, Milton, Bunyan, Scott, Butler, and Walton. The fourth and last buttress illustrates various professions, as suggested in the statues of Herbert, Livingstone, More, Jenner, Gresham, and Sir John Franklin.

The grouping of all the figures is most historic and instructive as representing the place and power of Great Britain in the world. These ideas are accentuated in the statues first, of founders and champions; second, in the builders up of Church and State; third, the promoters of the National Bible and Prayer Book; and fourth, the leaders of great movements in the spiritual, intellectual, and social world. Such a splendid array of human endeavor should be an inspiration to the youth of England. The floral ornamentation of the Reredos throughout is rendered highly symbolical by the graceful use of the emblems of the rose, thistle, shamrock, leek, oak, and vine. As a whole the Reredos is regarded as one of the most beautiful examples of perpendicular Gothic in modern times.

ALTAR AND REREDOS IN ST. GEORGE'S CHAPEL, WINDSOR

ST. GEORGE'S CHAPEL, WINDSOR

The Reredos constructed of alabaster was erected in the years 1862–63. It was provided by the Dean and Chapter at a cost of £1200. It was executed by an ecclesiastical sculptor named Philip from designs by Sir George Gilbert Scott. It was completed in time for the marriage of the present King Edward VII in March, 1863. The central subject represents the eleven disciples offering their adorations to the resurrected Lord. In one of the side panels Christ is instructing a group of his disciples and in the other he is appearing to St. Mary. These three panels are made in white marble. The panels on either side of the Reredos with the angel heads were added later, as also the rich canopy with its row of statues. At either end is the figure of St. George and the Dragon. These additions were put up in 1867 as a memorial to the Prince Consort.

ST. MATTHEW'S CHURCH, NORTHAMPTON

The Parish Souvenir for 1902 contains the following account:—

"Raised upon a marble foot-piece, eight steps from the nave floor, and placed some distance from the east wall of the apse, is the Altar, composed chiefly of wood, but with an alabaster front, which is divided into three main compartments, surrounded with moulded framing; and the compartments, of which the centre is the widest, are treated in sunk and moulded panel-work and tracery, beneath which are figure subjects in sculptured relief as follows: In the centre is the Feeding of the Multitude, in which Our Lord is represented as distributing the loaves and fishes to the disciples, and the disciples to the multitude. The men are seated on the ground according to the gospel story, while the women and children are seen standing on the outskirts of the throng. Below is inscribed the appropriate text —'If I send them away fasting, they will faint by the way.' The compartments on each side have typical subjects taken from the Old Testament. On the left hand is shown Melchizedek giving bread and wine to the patriarch Abraham, with the inscription, 'A Priest of the Most High God.' On the right hand is shown the angel appearing to Elijah under the juniper tree, with the inscription — 'Arise and eat, for the journey is too great for thee.'

"The whole of the sculptures are parcel gilt, and the backgrounds and mouldings are in gold and delicate colors. They are the work of Mr. W. Aumonier, of New Inn Yard, Tottenham Court Road, London.

"A Retable, or Gradine, of moulded and polished alabaster is built up from the floor of the apse at some clear distance east of the Altar, and from it rises the Reredos to a height of sixteen feet. The general composition is an arrangement of figure subjects in tiers and under canopies, with gables and intervening buttresses, and headed work running horizontally in the lowest stage. The central compartment contains the Crucifixion, with St. Mary and St. John; and arranged on either side are two tiers of saints and martyrs, chosen from all ages and some with reference to Church history of our own country. They are: St. Stephen, St. Ignatius, St. Polycarp, St. Vincent, St. Lawrence, St. Alban, St. George, St. Edmund, St. Giles, St. Columba, St. David, and St. Patrick. Below are female saints: St. Mary Magdalene, St. Lucy, St. Agnes, St. Margaret, and St. Helena."

ALTAR AND REREDOS IN ST. MATTHEW'S CHURCH, NORTHAMPTON

ALTAR AND REREDOS IN BEVERLEY MINSTER

By permission of F. Frich & Co., Reigate.

BEVERLEY MINSTER

In the *York Diocesan Magazine* for July, 1897, there appears an account of the restoration of the Altar Screen of Beverley Minster from the pen of the Rev. Canon Nolloth. This enters so decidedly into all the details of the work, and gives such an exhaustive description of the various statues, that it is by permission reprinted in full.

"The Reredos or Altar Screen of Beverley Minster has just been restored by the Vicar as a memorial to his father, the late Captain H. O. Nolloth, R.N. It was erected in 1826, and was an exact restoration of the old Screen which was constructed in the reign of Henry III and was defaced by the reforming zeal of the Puritans under Cromwell. The design contained two stages, each divided into twenty-four niches, those on the lower compartment having crocketed pediments, while the niches in the upper story are surmounted by beautiful tabernacle work, and on the top is an open battlement. The whole of these forty-eight niches and panels have been filled with mosaics and statues, the former by Messrs. Powell, and the latter by Mr. N. Hitch, of Vauxhall. The work has been exceedingly well designed and carried out, and the effect is such that the Altar Screen will henceforth be one of the greatest attractions of the interior of the Church. In the base of the Screen, below the two statues on the extreme right, the following inscription has been incised in Gothic letters:—

AD MAJ: DEI GLOR: ET IN MEMORIAM DILECTISSIMAM HENRICI OVENDEN NOLLOTH, IN CLASSE REGALI NUPER PRAEFECTI, PONUNTUR IN HOC PARIETE STATUAE ET MUSIVUM A.D. MDCCCXCVII.	Translated:— To the Glory of God and to the beloved memory of Henry Ovenden Nolloth, late Commander in the Royal Navy, the Statues and Mosaics are placed in this Screen A.D. 1897.

"At a short service held in the Choir of the Beverley Minster, on Tuesday evening, the Vicar, the Rev. Canon Nolloth, D.D., gave a description of the work, together with an account of the saints, kings, and ecclesiastics commemorated in it from their connection with Beverley and the north of England. The service began with the hymn 'Hark, the sound of Holy Voices.'

"The Vicar at this point said: —

"'The completion of the Reredos or Altar Screen was chosen as the subject of this memorial to one the last years of whose long and happy life were spent here, for two reasons: First, because it obviously appeared to be the work needing most to be taken in hand in the interior of the Minster — the one object in this Choir unsurpassed in beauty by any in Christendom, which seemed bare and unworthy, and yet occupying the most conspicuous position therein, the very focus of all its hallowed associations; and secondly, because of the danger that one day it might be taken in hand after the manner of a design which I have seen, without due consideration either of the historic and sacred interest which might be thrown into it, or of the paramount importance of harmonizing it with its surroundings. In saying this I am not unmindful that he who has ventured to attempt this task may possibly be held by not a few to have fallen a victim to this very danger, and to have failed in his high aim. For where architectural, antiquarian, and artistic tastes are all concerned, as in this instance, it were idle to imagine that all will approve. The author of this work can only reply that matters of this kind have been to him objects of deep interest and study and much travel all his life; that for the seventeen years of his sojourn in Beverley this work of restoration has been frequently in his mind, and he has had from time to time the opportunity of unfolding his views to, and having them approved by, many persons of high taste and culture.

"'The Reredos was erected about the year 1330, some eight or ten years apparently before the Percy Shrine. The eastern side of it, fronting the Chapel of St. John of Beverley (or, as it is now commonly but erroneously called, the "Lady Chapel"), remains very much in its original condition, with the two beautiful niches, "waving" string course, and delicate ornamentation which made Rickman declare it to be "the best school for decorated details in England." The Screen was intended to separate the Choir with its constant services from interruption by the stream of pilgrims and diseased persons visiting the shrine of St. John of Beverley, who was described by Professor Bright as "an object of greater reverence than any northern saint, except Cuthbert." The gallery on the top of it would probably contain a diminutive "pair of organs," possibly a Rood; and behind the Rood a cell of carved woodwork for the watcher of the shrine. The front of it is that with which we have to do. At the dissolution of the society of St. John, in 1547, or probably soon after, the statuary was broken down, and the rich tabernacle-work defaced. Later it was covered with a coating of plaster, on which the Commandments, the Lord's Prayer, and the Apostles' Creed were rudely painted. In the beginning of the last century a high and incongruous Screen of oak, with eight Corinthian columns supporting a triumphal arch, surmounted by a gilded eagle, the emblem of St. John the Evangelist, was erected in front of it. About 1815 the upper part of this Screen, which was so high as to block out the view of nearly the whole of the east window, was taken down, leaving its huge pedestal. Mr. Comins, the clever master mason then employed at the Minster, carefully examined the mutilated remains of the ancient Reredos, took casts of the ornaments and mouldings, and persuaded the trustees that it was practicable to restore it in all its details. This was done, and completed in February, 1826. Plenty of fragments of every part of the original work remain which show that the reproduction was most careful and exact.

"'But in this state the Screen was after all only a series of twelve niches without the statues, and thirty-six frames without the pictures. Its abundant, rich carving was only noticed by the close observer, and its effect from the body of the Choir was that of a stone wall, relieved only by a pierced parapet. The problem was, how best to reproduce the combined effect of statuary with gold and color in the original: and at the same time to make it tell something of the history of the kings and great men who had to do with the bringing of Christianity into these parts in the days of old, and of the saints of Holy Writ.

"'In the centre were twelve flat panels, showing that the Twelve Apostles were represented above the altar, as at St. Alban's, Bampton, and Bridlington Priory. On either side were six niches for statues, which, from the evidence of other figures and carved heads which remain here, and from the general practice of mediæval sculpture in this country, would contain statues of saints and worthies of more or less local renown. Over the whole are twenty-four shorter panels, twelve narrow and twelve wider. The Twelve Apostles have therefore been replaced in the centre in mosaic by Messrs. Powell, who have executed the great mosaic work at St. Paul's and elsewhere, and by long study and experiment have succeeded in producing much of the effect of the old Italian work. The vermilion and gold diaper of the ground is a reproduction of the ancient pattern which was discovered by carefully washing a piece of the old stonework. It corresponds with the carved rose diaper of the pilasters.

"'The twelve statues, six on either side of the Apostles, were intrusted to Mr. Hitch, of Vauxhall, on account of his great experience of such work under Mr. J. L. Pearson, the eminent R.A. and architect of Truro Cathedral, and many important churches, including Dalton Holme in this neighborhood. Mr. Hitch had executed the figures in the Altar Screens of Truro Cathedral and New College Oxford, and figures at Peterborough and Lincoln Cathedrals, etc. Mr. Pearson has most carefully superintended the execution of these figures, Beverley Minster and this Screen having been familiar to him from youth. Full-sized clay models of all the statues were approved by him, and an exact model of the niches made for the purpose. He had the small bases on which the figures rest modeled and altered three if not four times over, ideas for them being supplied by drawings of bases in other parts of the Minster. With Mr. Pearson's full approval the niches have been lined with mosaic of the same ancient pattern. This has the twofold advantage of throwing the figures into bold relief and securing uniformity of tone by carrying the effect of gold and color over the whole Screen. I am not aware of any other instance of this treatment in England, but it is to be met with in Italy, notably in a fine example at Ravenna.

"'Let me here turn aside to deal with one or two criticisms. It may be asked: Does not the second Commandment prohibit "graven images"? Yes, but only when made to be "bowed down to" and "worshipped." This is clear from the words which follow, "nor the likeness of anything that is in the heaven above, or in the earth beneath," which would, if unlimited, render it equally wrong to take a photographic likeness of your nearest relative. In the Jewish Tabernacle itself, there were figures of cherubim made by command of God Himself: so was the brazen serpent. But when, long afterwards, the Israelites offered incense to it, Hezekiah ground it to powder. The same abuse brought the same fate upon the statues with which our Cathedrals and Minsters were adorned three centuries ago; and we can scarcely blame, though we may deplore, the destructive zeal of our Puritan forefathers.'

"The Vicar then proceeded to deal at length with other possible objections; pointing out the need of some warmth and color, and the difficulty of introducing it. He said he hoped that by confining it to the sunk portions, the rich carving of the rest of the Screen would be thrown into relief as it never was before, and at the same time a disastrous contrast with the Percy Shrine would be avoided.

"In the central mosaics each Apostle bears his emblem — St. Peter the keys, St. Andrew his cross, etc. In the twelve panels above an angel displays over each Apostle a scroll inscribed with the portion of the Creed traditionally assigned to him. In the fifteenth-century glass preserved in the upper portion of the east window, Apostles are seen bearing the scrolls themselves.

"The twelve statues represent: —

"1. King Lucius. The register of Simon Russell, a valuable manuscript of the date 1416, commonly known as the 'Provost's Book,' and now happily restored to the Minster, commences with the statement that Lucius, son of Coil, founded the Church of Beverley in the year 187. As the story of Lucius, and his foundation of churches in London, Gloucester, and elsewhere, is generally regarded as apocryphal, this apparent sanction of it has been condemned by some critics. But as Archbishop Usher gives a list of no less than twenty-three authorities who mention him, and as the story was current in both the Celtic and Saxon branches of the Church in Britain, there seems no reason to doubt that there was a British chief of that name who became Christian. Even if we regard him as purely legendary, it seems to me that legend has as legitimate a place in the sculpture of a Gothic Minster, 'a poem in stone,' as in the verse of Tennyson. If he be entirely a myth, then his figure as the founder in primitive crown and armor, and bearing the model of a very early Church in his hand, may be taken as the embodiment of a fact — that the foundation of this venerable sanctuary goes back beyond the historic period into the realm of legend.

"2. St. Hilda, Abbess of Whitby; preceptress of St. John of Beverley.

"3. St. John of Beverley, born at Harpham-on-the-Wolds; sent as a boy to the school of Canterbury, taught by the African Hadrian, the fellow-laborer of Archbishop Theodore, of Tarsus. From Canterbury John passed to Whitby. No less than five students under Hilda, this mother in Israel, became Bishops of various Sees. On Sunday, August 25, 687, John was consecrated Bishop of Hexham, nineteen years after he was translated to York. He was a true missionary Bishop, a light shining in a dark place, preaching the Gospel from an open Bible, as portrayed in that figure, and always surrounded by a little band of scholars whom he trained for evangelistic work. His skill in medicine, which, with mathematics, astronomy, and music, as well as theology, he had learned in the school at Canterbury, enabled him to perform cures which in those simple days were thought miraculous. Most of us remember the story of his treatment of the deaf and dumb youth. In the year 718, he retired to Beverley, where he had rebuilt the Church, and founded, not as commonly reported, a monastery, as that term is now understood, but a half parochial, half missionary establishment, to be a centre of light and Christian teaching in the forest of Deira. Three years later he died, and was buried in what was then the apse of St. Peter, now the east end of the Nave.

"4. Brithunus, disciple of St. John, and first Abbot of Beverley; buried in the Minster near him. The ancient sixth bell, formerly the second, cast about the year 1366, bears this inscription: —

"'Ista secunda tonat ut plus Brithunus ametur.'

"5. The Venerable Bede, disciple and biographer of St. John of Beverley, by whom he was ordained deacon and priest; a learned man of science and historian. He finished the translation of the gospels into Anglo-Saxon, which St. John had begun. It is almost impossible to exaggerate the influence which he exercised upon the learning of the early Middle Ages. No less remarkable was his piety and humility. Time would fail to mention the beautiful stories treasured in his ecclesiastical history. Various explanations are given of the origin of his being called 'The Venerable.' (Two of these were related.) The story of his death is minutely told by an eye-witness. It occurred on the eve of Ascension Day, in the year 735. Shortly before, he had composed an antiphon which seems to have been the original of our Collect for the Sunday after Ascension Day: 'O King of Glory, Lord of might, who didst on this day triumphantly ascend far above the heavens, we beseech Thee, leave us not comfortless, but send to us the promise of the Father, even the Spirit of Truth, Hallelujah.'

"6. King Athelstan; bearing in one hand the dagger, which he left as a pledge on the Altar here, and which is still preserved with the remains of St. John, and in the other his famous charter to the Church of Beverley, on which are seen the words ALS FRE.

"7. Eborius, first recorded Bishop of York, 314.

"8. St. Gregory the Great. In the west window of the south aisle you may remember how he is displayed walking through the slave market at Rome, and struck by the three fair children, who are said to have been sons of a Prince of Holderness, a district into which our parish extends: 'Call them not Angles, but Angels,' he said (non Anglos, sed Angelos). Asking the region whence they were brought, he was told 'Deira.' 'Then will we deliver them from the wrath (de irâ) of God.' He never forgot his vow, and when he became Bishop, soon sent St. Augustine to our shores. He is represented frequently, as in this figure, with a dove whispering into his ear: The emblem of inspiration.

"9. St. Augustine of Canterbury.

"10. St. Alured of Beverley. A great historian. 'The English Florus.' Born at Beverley, 1109; Sacristan, Canon, and Treasurer of the Minster. Afterwards Abbot of Rievaulx. One of the Saints of the Cistercian Order; his day the 2d of March.

"11. Ethelberga, a Christian Princess of Kent, married to

"12. Eadwine, King of Northumbria, by Paulinus, 625. Edwin was baptized Easter Eve, 627.

"Paulinus appears in the second panel of the upper tier of mosaics. He was the first Saxon Bishop of York, 627.

"Coifi, the last High Priest of Thor. Converted by Paulinus at Goodmanham, he was the first to cast his spear at the old sacred enclosure of the Temple and trample his idols under foot. Bede has preserved for us the story of the Northumbrian thane, who, when King Edwin at this same Conference at Goodmanham asked his council to decide whether the missionary Paulinus should be heard, gave his voice for Christianity, for he said the human soul seemed to him like the little bird which fluttered in winter into a lighted hall, and then out again into darkness. No one knew whence it came, and whither it went. 'This man says that he can tell us. Let us hear him.'

"Alchfrid, King of Northumbria, by whom St. John of Beverley was made Bishop of Hexham.

"St. Wilfrid, Bishop of York, 665.

"St. Chad, Bishop of York, and afterwards of Lichfield, reversing the order of our own Diocesan.

"Winwald, disciple of St. John of Beverley, and second Abbot, 733. Buried in the Minster.

"Alcuin, preceptor of Charlemagne, Canon and Chancellor of York: a link between Bede and the learning of the Middle Ages.

"Kinsius, Archbishop of York, 1051; he built a high tower to the Church of Beverley, and placed in it two great bells, which are seen above him, while he holds the model of the tower in his hand.

"St. William of York, Archbishop, 1144.

"St. Thomas à Becket, Provost of Beverley, 1139; Archbishop of Canterbury, 1162; murdered in Canterbury Cathedral, 1178.

"At either end of this row is placed a subject appropriate to him to whose memory this work is dedicated. At the north end appears

St. Nicholas, Bishop of Myra, the Patron of sailors, said to have quelled by his prayers a violent storm in the Mediterranean; his hand rests upon an anchor. In almost every seaport, and near many a riverside, as at Beverley, was to be found once a Church bearing his name. The south end closes the entire series with the old ecclesiastical emblem — the 'Navis,' or 'Ship of the Church'; over her bulwark hangs another ancient symbol, an anchor enclosed within a circle, suggestive of eternal hope. Almost from the time when a little vessel, tossing upon the Sea of Galilee, bore the Redeemer of the world and the twelve Apostles, we find this symbol in ecclesiastical imagery. 'The Church,' says an old father, 'is like a ship, bearing over the unquiet sea mariners from every clime, but all bound for one haven.' We find the same thought in Charles Wesley's hymn: —

> " 'There all the ship's company meet,
> Who sailed with the Saviour beneath.' "

CHRISTCHURCH PRIORY, HANTS

THIS is an ancient stone Reredos, probably earlier than the fifteenth century. It is arranged into three tiers with five compartments in each, the central one wider than those on either side. The Reredos is carved with a representation of the tree of Jesse. The Rev. Thomas Perkins writes: "Above the Altar in the central compartment Jesse lies asleep; on the left hand David plays upon his harp; on the right sits Solomon deeply meditating. Above Jesse we have in one carving an amalgamated representation of the birth of Christ and the visit of the Wise Men. On the left hand sits the Virgin Mary with her Child, fully clothed in a long garment, not wrapped in swaddling clothes, standing in her lap. Behind her stands a man, probably Joseph, and before her kneels one of the Wise Men, offering his gift of gold in the form of a plain tankard. On the right behind him stand his two fellows, one carrying a pot of myrrh, the other a boat-shaped vessel, probably intended for a censer containing frankincense. On a bracket above the head of the kneeling Wise Man, the shepherds kneel in adoration; nor are the flocks that they were tending forgotten, for several sheep may be seen on a hilltop above their heads. Thirty-two small figures may be counted in niches in the buttresses dividing the compartments. Crockets, finials, and pinnacles decorate the various canopies over the carvings."[1]

[1] *Wimborne Minster and Christchurch Priory*, pp. 112–113.

By permission of Rev. Thomas H. Bush, M.A.

ALTAR AND SCREEN IN CHRISTCHURCH PRIORY, HANTS

By permission of Cyril Ellis, London.

ALTAR AND REREDOS IN THE CHAPEL OF THE CONVENT OF ST. MARGARET, EAST GRINSTEAD

CHAPEL OF THE CONVENT OF ST. MARGARET, EAST GRINSTEAD

Both Altar and Reredos are built of beautifully polished material. The Altar is built of alabaster at a cost of £150. The Reredos is also of polished alabaster with panels containing figures in marble. The middle one represents the Crucifixion of our Lord, with four others of scenes in Scripture story. The Reredos cost $1000, and with the Altar was built by Earp and Hobbs, Lambeth, London.

ST. STEPHEN'S CHURCH, CLEWER

THE Reredos was built in 1875 by Mr. Woodyear, and the decorations were executed by Mr. George Ostrehan, brother of the Vicar. The central figure is that of Christ holding the cross in his right hand and an orb in his left. The highly polished material and the graceful proportions make the Reredos very effective. The Altar is constructed of oak with mensa of stone. On the front are representations of the nine orders of angels, finished in gold and color.

ALTAR AND REREDOS IN THE CHURCH OF ST. STEPHEN, CLEWER

ALTAR AND REREDOS IN THE CHURCH OF ST. MARGARET, KING'S LYNN

ST. MARGARET'S CHURCH, KING'S LYNN

THE Reredos is a fine illustration of artistic carving in wood. It was erected at a cost of £1000. That sum was left for the purpose by Miss Blencome of Lynn. The material used is carved oak, painted and gilded. The design was made by Mr. Bodley and executed by Mr. Bridgeman of Lichfield. The central figure is that of Our Blessed Lord. On his right hand and left are figures of St. Jerome, St. Augustine, St. Ambrose, and St. Gregory.

CHURCH OF ST. MARY MAGDALENE, ELMSTONE, CHELTENHAM

In the issue of the *Gloucestershire Chronicle* for September 25, 1886, there is an account of a thanksgiving service in the Church of St. Mary Magdalene on the festival of St. Matthew. It reads: —

"The main feature of the day was, however, the benediction of a new Reredos, erected under a faculty issued by the Chancellor of the Diocese, and by the munificence of two parishioners (the Misses Holt), at a cost of £150. The Reredos consists of three principal and six subsidiary compartments. The central compartment, which is projected somewhat forward, and so breaks the ordinarily monotonous straight line which is characteristic of most Reredoses, springs from a base on which, in the midst of rich diaper work, are carved the sacred letters 'I. H. S.' Above this base, and deeply recessed, is a crucifix in bas-relief, with, at its foot, figures of St. Mary and St. John, also in bas-relief. Above is a canopy, surmounted by a spire of crocketing work, terminating in a finial. A similar but smaller spire surmounts the other two principal compartments, — that on the north side being occupied by an image of the Blessed Virgin, holding the Divine Child; that on the south by an image of St. George, the treatment of which is strikingly original and effective, a sword taking the place of the conventional spear, and the convolutions of the dragon exhibiting great vigor of treatment. The six subsidiary compartments are occupied, on the south side of the central compartment, by images of St. Augustine of Hippo, St. Mary Magdalene, the patron saint of the Church, and St. Ambrose; on the north side by the images of St. Gregory, St. Alphege of Deerhurst (Elmstone Church being an offshoot of that religious house), and St. Jerome. The images and the Crucifixion group are of Seaton stone, the pure white of which contrasts most effectively with the deeper tint of the fine Corsham stone of which the rest of the Reredos is composed. Each image stands upon a carved capital, and the pillars of the arcading are of red Mansfield stone. The general line of the top of the

ALTAR AND REREDOS IN THE CHURCH OF ST. MARY MAGDALENE, ELMSTONE

Reredos consists of perforated and richly carved cresting. The gradines are of white alabaster, capped with Sicilian marble, and exquisitely carved with passion flowers, ears of corn, vine leaves, and grapes. The bases of the two extreme compartments are richly diapered. The Altar rails, presented by the churchwardens, are of alabaster, combined with Seaton stone, and supported by alabaster bases, shafts, and capitals. The whole was designed and executed by Mr. A. B. Wall, of Cheltenham, who is to be congratulated upon the completion of a Reredos which will add greatly to the reputation which he already enjoys, not merely in his own locality but throughout the kingdom. Independently of the stately beauty of the design as a whole, the Reredos is remarkable for the unusual excellency of its carving, the expression and pose of the images, and a conscientious care, even in the most minute details, which deserves the highest praise."

CHRIST CHURCH, BRISTOL

The Church of St. Ewen stood for many years opposite Christ Church, but in 1787 the two livings were consolidated. St. Ewen's was demolished in 1820. The Reredos was constructed of stone in 1883. The central panel is a representation of the Crucifixion. In a niche on the right is a figure of St. Ewen. The niche on the left contains a statue of St. John the Baptist. The south aisle of St. Ewen's was dedicated to St. John the Baptist and was the Chapel of the Merchant Tailors' Guild. The four heads, two above and two near the ground, in the Reredos represent four Latin Fathers. Above are reliefs of angels with censers. The Reredos is a memorial. Toward its erection Mrs. Cole and the Misses Cole, the then Rector's mother and sisters, gave £100, in memory of Thomas Bulman Cole. The entire cost of the Reredos was £180.

By permission of Cyril Ellis, London.

ALTAR AND REREDOS IN CHRIST CHURCH, BRISTOL

By permission of Cyril Ellis, London.

ST. PAUL'S CHURCH, CLIFTON, BRISTOL

THE Reredos is built of teakwood, while the base is of marble and the sides of alabaster. The three pictures represent the revival of an ancient art. A good and rich glass is subjected to great heat, and then it is painted on. Again it is submitted to heat with the result that the colors are burned in and the work becomes permanent. It is an improvement on the old mosaics, inasmuch as the human face and form are more natural and graceful. Messrs. Powell of Whitefriars designed and executed the pictures, and Mr. Henry Hirst of Bristol was the architect. The central panel represents the glorified Christ. As our great High Priest he is represented as blessing the congregation. The crucified Lord is on the left, and the Nativity on the right. The whole design of the Reredos is to accentuate the doctrines of the Atonement and the Incarnation. The Reredos was finished in September, 1903, and with the other decorations of the sanctuary was the gift of Mr. George White, of Bristol, commemorating his daughter's marriage in the Church. The cost of the Reredos was £1000, while £350 more were spent on the adjacent enrichments.

CHURCH OF ST. MARY'S, REDCLIFFE BRISTOL

THE Reredos is modern, having been erected in 1866–67. It was designed by Mr. Godwin, the architect of the Church. All except the three middle panels was carved by Mr. Rice. The whole of the Altar and Reredos is of Caen stone. The central panel is Christ blessing the loaves and the fishes. The panel on the right hand represents the distribution of the loaves and the one on the left the distribution of the fishes. These three panels were carved in London out of very fine Caen stone. The cost of the entire work was about £1000.

ALTAR AND REREDOS IN THE CHURCH OF ST. MARY, REDCLIFFE, BRISTOL

By permission of Cyril Ellis, London.

ALTAR AND REREDOS IN ST. CHAD'S CHURCH, HAGGERSTON

CHURCH OF ST. CHAD, HAGGERSTON

THE Altar is of massive oak, with a stone slab. It was presented by Mr. J. Scott Chad, of Thurstone Hall, Norfolk. The Reredos was erected in 1889. It is constructed of white stone inlaid with marble. The architect was Mr. Brooks and the sculptor was Mr. Earp, of Lambeth. The figures in the centre of the Reredos represent Our Lord on the Cross, while at his feet are the Blessed Virgin Mary and St. John. On the right hand are Joseph of Arimathea and the Roman Centurion. On the left are St. Mary Magdalene and St. Mary, wife of Cleophas. The Reredos was the gift of several friends, but is not a memorial. The foundation stone of St. Chad's Church was laid by the late Rt. Rev. Charles T. Quintard, D.D., L.L.D., M.D., Bishop of Tennessee, on Shrove Tuesday, February 25, 1868.

CHURCH OF ST. MARY THE VIRGIN, MARSH GIBBON

The Altar is built of oak and was erected in 1880. A carved stone Reredos reaching the length of the Altar was added in 1902. It represents the institution of the Holy Communion. Our Lord is standing in the act of blessing the cup, and surrounded by the Apostles. A border of vine leaves and grapes surrounds the whole. At the same time a painted east window was constructed. The Reredos and window were dedicated by the Lord Bishop of Oxford at a special service on October 20, 1902. The cost of the Reredos and window was £170. The Reredos was executed by Earp and Hobbs and the window by Heaton, Butler, and Bayne, of London.

By permission of Henry W. Taunt & Co., Oxford.
ALTAR AND REREDOS IN THE CHURCH OF ST. MARY THE VIRGIN, MARSH GIBBON

ALTAR AND REREDOS IN ST. PETER'S CHAPEL OF BURFORD CHURCH

ST. PETER'S CHAPEL OF BURFORD CHURCH

The Reredos is an antique structure dating from about 1490. It is built of stone with a canopy of wood. A figure of Our Blessed Lord is in the centre, with the Virgin Mary on his right hand and St. Dorothea, virgin and martyr, on his left. These were the Christian names of two sisters who restored the Chapel in memory of a sister. The topmost figure represents St. Peter, which was found under the floor of the nave at the restoration in 1872. The figures were carved in London, but the name of the artist is unknown. The same can be said of the original builder. The architect of the restoration was Mr. G. E. Street. The cost of this, which included the coloring of stone and woodwork, was £74.10.

MINSTER LOVELL, WITNEY

The Reredos is of white stone, and was erected in 1876 in memory of Lady Maria Taunton. It consists of five panels. Starting from the left we have the Annunciation, the Nativity, the Crucifixion, the Resurrection, and the Ascension.

ALTAR AND REREDOS IN MINSTER LOVELL, WITNEY

By permission of Mr. W. Adams, Witney.

ALTAR AND REREDOS IN ST. MARY'S CHURCH, WITNEY

ST. MARY'S CHURCH, WITNEY

The Reredos is of stone and was erected in 1884. The statues are of alabaster, delicately accentuated with gold. The Saviour is represented in the central group, with an angel on either side. The other figures placed in recesses are the Blessed Virgin Mary, St. John, St. Mary Magdalene, and St. Peter. The whole symbolizes the doctrine of Our Lord's Resurrection, and leads up to the further scriptural truths in the painted window above. The work is a memorial, as indicated by the following inscription: "To the glory of God, and in memory of Augustine Batt, M.D., son of Edward Augustine Batt, surgeon." The Reredos was built by Clayton and Bell, and Mr. Nicholls was the sculptor. The cost was between £300 and £400.

CHURCH OF ST. JOHN THE BAPTIST, CIRENCESTER

The Reredos was erected in 1867, and later, in 1889, was colored and gilded. The architect was Sir George Gilbert Scott, and the sculptor was G. E. Geflowski, Brinton Street, London. The material used is stone. The central panel represents the Agony, the Crucifixion, and the Resurrection of our Lord. The side panels to the north represent the Annunciation and the preaching of St. John the Baptist. Those to the south the Nativity of Christ and his Baptism. The figures in the niches are the four Evangelists with their symbols.

ALTAR AND REREDOS IN THE CHURCH OF ST. JOHN THE BAPTIST, CIRENCESTER

ALTAR AND REREDOS IN HOLY TRINITY CHURCH, WATERMOOR

By permission of Henry W. Taunt & Co., Oxford.

HOLY TRINITY CHURCH, WATERMOOR

THE Altar was erected in 1851, and the Reredos in 1881. Sculptured freestone is the material used, with columns in marble. The central panel represents Our Lord in glory. On one side is the Entombment of Christ, and on the other the Women at the Tomb after the Resurrection. The sculptor was Mr. Geflowski, and the builder, Mr. Bridges, of Cirencester. The architect was Sir George Gilbert Scott. The work was subscribed for by the ladies of the parish.

CHURCH OF ST. JOHN THE BAPTIST, SUMMERTOWN

The Reredos was erected during the time that the late Archbishop of Capetown was Vicar of the parish. The material used is stone, which is constructed in three panels. The central one is a representation in relief of the Crucifixion. On one side of the figure on the Cross stands St. Mary the Virgin, and on the other side St. John. At the foot of the Cross is the figure of St. Mary Magdalene. The two side panels are rich in mosaic work.

ALTAR AND REREDOS IN CHURCH OF ST. JOHN THE BAPTIST, SUMMERTOWN

ALTAR AND REREDOS IN ALL SAINTS' CHURCH, EVESHAM

By permission of Henry W. Taunt & Co., Oxford.

ALL SAINTS' CHURCH, EVESHAM

This Church was built by the monks in the time of Edward III, shortly after the battle of Cressy, in memory of those who fell; hence the name of the Church. It was connected with an Abbey founded in 701 by the Bishop of Worcester, who resigned his see and became the first Abbot. The Reredos is modern and was built in 1876, at a cost of £130, and is of marble. The central part depicts the Descent from the Cross. The side panels contain angels in the attitude of worship. The architect was E. Purdy, of London, and the builder, R. L. Boulton, of Cheltenham. The Reredos was the gift of the Holland family. The Altar is of oak and was erected sometime before 1870.

ST. MARY'S CHURCH, STREATLEY

The Reredos was erected in 1893, and is constructed of alabaster. The central panel represents Our Lord on the Cross, with St. John and the Virgin Mary on either side. The panel on the Epistle side contains the Resurrection and on the Gospel side the Holy Family. The figures in the canopies are the four Evangelists and Moses and Aaron. The work was erected as a memorial to Mrs. Stone of Streatley Hall. Mr. Pearson was the architect, and the builder and sculptor was Mr. Hitch, of Vauxhall. The cost was about £200.

ALTAR AND REREDOS IN THE CHURCH OF ST. MARY, STREATLEY

By permission of Henry W. Taunt & Co., Oxford.

ALTAR AND TRIPTYCH IN ALL SAINTS' CHURCH, RICHARD'S CASTLE, LUDLOW

By permission of Cyril Ellis, London.

ALL SAINTS' CHURCH, RICHARD'S CASTLE, LUDLOW

The Altar and Triptych were erected in 1892–93. The central compartment represents the Crucifixion, and the side panels contain St. Mary and St. John. The panel on the Epistle side has the figures of St. James and St. Peter, and that on the Gospel side of St. Catherine and St. Cecilia. The panels on the extreme right and left contain adoring angels. The Triptych is one of the finest examples of the noted artist, Charles E. Buckeridge. The architect was Norman Shaw. The cost was about £800.

CHRIST CHURCH, READING

THE Reredos was erected in 1862–63. It is constructed of Caen stone, with forest of Dean shafts. The central representation is that of the Ascension. The eleven disciples are arranged in groups, two groups on either side of Christ. The sculptor was Mr. Thomas Nicholls. The designer of the Reredos was Mr. Burnie Philips, the architect the late Mr. Henry Woodyear, and the builders Messrs. Wheeler Bros., of Reading. The spaces on the east wall on either side of the Reredos are filled with frescoes executed by Heaton, Butler, and Bayne in 1897.

ALTAR AND REREDOS IN CHRIST CHURCH, READING

By permission of Henry W. Taunt & Co., Oxford.

ALTAR IN THE CRYPT OF THE CATHEDRAL OF ST. JOHN THE DIVINE, NEW YORK CITY

CATHEDRAL OF ST. JOHN THE DIVINE, NEW YORK CITY

THIS Altar was exhibited at the World's Columbian Exposition in 1893. Afterward it was purchased by Mrs. Celia W. Wallace, of Chicago, and presented to the Cathedral of St. John the Divine, New York, and there placed in the crypt, where daily services are now held. This remarkable example of mosaic work was designed by Mr. Louis C. Tiffany. There are nearly one million pieces of opalescent glass, pearl, and semi-precious stones used in its construction. The Altar is composed of mosaic and white marble, with the monogram of the Holy Name and the Apocalyptic emblems of the Evangelists in mosaics of mother-of-pearl and semi-precious stones. The Retable carries an inscription in mosaic from the sixth chapter of the Gospel of St. John, relating to the Eucharistic office. The door of the tabernacle is of filigree metal work enriched with gems and semi-precious stones. The Reredos is of iridescent glass mosaic, the design being the vine, symbolical of the Sacrament of the Eucharist, and the Peacock, a symbol of immortality. The Ciborium consists of a series of arches, the faces of which are covered with ornaments in relief, with overlays of gold and settings of glass jewels, and inlays of mosaic inscriptions. These arches are supported by columns, composed entirely of mosaic, and contain over two hundred thousand pieces of glass. The Predella is approached by a series of steps with risers of glass mosaic bearing inscriptions from the Psalms of David. From the floor of the Chapel to the Predella are five steps, symbolizing the five wounds of Our Lord and Saviour. The three upper steps upon which the Predella and the Altar rest are typical of the Holy Trinity, the foundation of the faith.

This account was chiefly supplied by the Tiffany Co.

CHRIST CHURCH CATHEDRAL, LOUISVILLE, KY.

THE Reredos is seventeen feet high in the centre and thirteen feet six inches on the sides. It is divided into seven panels with shafts that support arches. The three larger ones contain niches crowned by gabled canopies. These contain statues of Our Blessed Lord in the attitude of benediction, with the Virgin Mother on the one side and St. John on the other, all carved of white statuary marble. The statues stand upon pedestals under richly cut canopies with a gold-colored background. The minor niches, four in number, are of Caen stone carved in relief with the passion flower, the lily, the wheat, and the vine. The Retable is of white statuary marble and has two gradines and a throne for the cross. The central panel under the cross has a chalice in relief, and the lower riser has on its face the ascription, " Holy, Holy, Holy, Lord God of Hosts." The shelving is of Piedmont marble, of a rich warm gray. The architect was Mr. Henry M. Congdon.

ALTAR AND REREDOS IN CHRIST CHURCH CATHEDRAL, LOUISVILLE, KY.

ALTAR AND REREDOS IN ALL SAINTS' CATHEDRAL, MILWAUKEE, WIS.

ALL SAINTS' CATHEDRAL, MILWAUKEE, WIS.

THE Altar and Reredos were erected in 1902. The material is white oak. The central statue is that of Our Lord, and St. Matthew and St. Luke with symbols are on his right and left. The statues were carved at Munich in Bavaria. The architects were Brielmaier and Sons, Milwaukee. They were also the builders.

CATHEDRAL OF ST. JOHN, QUINCY, ILLINOIS

THE following description, written by the Very Rev. Wyllys Rede, D.D., which appeared in *The Cathedral Chimes* for July, 1907, is reproduced with his consent: —

"Through the generosity of the family of the late Richard F. Newcomb, Esq., who was for many years an active member of the Cathedral congregation, we have now a Reredos in the Cathedral at Quincy worthy to rank with the best at home or abroad. It will at once be recognized by all competent critics as a work of the highest order both in design and execution. It is marked by great originality, beauty, and significance. Its purpose is not merely ornamental; it is intended to tell a most high and important story, to set forth some of the chief truths of our religion in such a way as to stimulate and assist devotion. It is pervaded by a feeling of exaltation, of aspiration, of solemn repose which is most worshipful. Although many minds and hands have been employed in its production, all its features are harmonized into a remarkable unity.

"The theme of the Reredos is 'The Final Harvest.' It is an attempt to express in painting and sculpture the teachings of Our Lord as to the consummation of our redemption. Its scriptural basis is found in St. Matthew xiii. 24–30 and 36–43. In this beautiful passage of Holy Scripture the great Teacher describes the gathering in of the harvest of souls at the end of the world,— the final harvest home. 'The field is the world; the harvest is the end of the world; and the reapers are the angels. This noble conception is worked out in the Reredos with great fullness and force.

"In the central painting are seen three bright and beauteous angels in mid-air, one bearing grapes, another wheat, the third bending over the earth to curse the tares. Behind and beneath them stretches a wide landscape of smoking ruins, crumbling towers, and tottering walls, sinking into the shadows cast by the lurid light of the last day. The skillful management of light and shade in this wonderful painting and its striking color effects are worthy of careful study. It is an

ALTAR AND REREDOS IN THE CATHEDRAL OF ST. JOHN, QUINCY, ILLINOIS

original creation and will rank high amongst the great paintings of America.

"Above this central scene and closely connected with it is another of exceeding interest and beauty. Enthroned in the clouds sits the Lord of the harvest, a majestic and benignant figure, waiting to receive the fruits of the harvest, which are being borne up to him by his angelic ministers. A refulgent, heavenly light streams down upon him, indicating the presence of the Father and his participation in the great harvest home together with that of the Holy Spirit, who hovers between in the form of a dove. Thus we have the three persons of the Holy Trinity joining in the consummation of our redemption — God the Father represented by the light from above, God the Son on the throne receiving the fruits of his redemption, and God the Holy Spirit as the agent in this great work. The Lord of the harvest is attended by a great company of saints and angels who have labored in the harvest field. Close about him is clustered a group of angels radiant with the joy and the triumph of the occasion, each of whom has the most marked individuality and should be closely studied. They blend into a wonderful harmony of coloring and add much to the impressiveness of the scene. In the buttresses at each side are other carved figures of angels bearing instruments of worship with which they celebrate the ingathering of the harvest. But they are not the only nor the chief attendants of the great King. This honor is reserved for the saints who by his incarnation and redemptive work have been united with him, some of whom appear in this Reredos as representatives of them all. First and foremost are the two who were most closely identified with him in his earthly ministry, — his Virgin Mother and the beloved disciple St. John. They stand at either side as witnesses and participants in the scene. The artist has pictured them in mature life, with the fair complexion which belonged to the descendants of the house of David, and in attitudes most striking and appropriate. Each of these paintings is a masterpiece, that of St. John being especially notable for power and originality.

"Across the base of the structure stretches an array of carved figures of saints representative of the laborers in the harvest field in all ages of the Church. In the centre stand four representatives of Apostolic times — on the left two Apostles to the Jews, St. Peter and St. James, and on the right two missionaries to the Gentiles, St. Paul and St. Barnabas. At the extreme left appear two great leaders of the undivided Church, St. Ambrose and St. Augustine. The corresponding position at the right is occupied by two great representatives of Anglican Christianity, one from ancient and the other from modern times, St. Anselm and John Keble. All these are exquisitely carved, and each of them exhibits a most striking individuality. Together they form a noble group of laborers in the harvest. As signs of the toil and suffering with which the harvest was gathered in, the marks of the Passion are seen near the summit of the Reredos. Attached to the central buttresses is the highly colored coat of arms of the Cathedral, and upon the outer buttresses that of the Diocese, both of these having been designed by the eminent authority in heraldry, Mr. Pierre de Chaignon la Rose, of Boston. The woodwork of the Reredos, which is of carved oak and is colored a soft grayish brown, was designed by Messrs. Cram, Goodhue, and Ferguson, of Boston, and executed by William F. Ross and Co., of Cambridge. The paintings are the work of the artist-priest, the Rev. Johannes A. Oertel, D.D., of Washington, D.C., a painter who works in the spirit of the old masters and whose canvasses enrich many of our churches."

The central painting has been valued at $5000. The cost of the rest of the work is stated at $3000. On July 7, 1907, being the sixth Sunday after Trinity, the Altar and Reredos received a benediction through Bishop Fawcett. He was assisted in the Holy Eucharist by Dean Rede and Canon Gustin, who acted as gospeller and epistoler. The sermon was preached by the Rev. Edward A. Larrabee, Rector of the Church of the Ascension, Chicago. He was a former Rector of St. John's Church at the time when it became the diocesan Cathedral.

ALTAR AND REREDOS IN TRINITY CHURCH, NEW YORK CITY

TRINITY CHURCH, NEW YORK CITY

The architect, Mr. Frederick Clarke Withers, furnishes the following description:—

"The memorial to the late William B. Astor, which has been erected by his two sons in Trinity Church, is in the form of an Altar and Reredos, the latter occupying nearly the whole width (thirty-five feet) of the Chancel, and carried up as high as the sill of the large seven-light window which is about twenty feet from the floor.

"The Altar is eleven feet long, and is constructed of pure white statuary marble, with shafts of Lisbon red marble supporting capitals carved in natural foliage dividing the front and side into panels. In the centre panel, which is carved with passion flowers, is a maltese cross in mosaic, set with cameos, a head of Our Lord being in the centre, and the symbols of the Evangelists at the extremities of the four arms; this panel is flanked by two kneeling angels, the one in adoration and the other in prayer. The other panels in front which are carved with ears of wheat are also in mosaic, and contain the 'Pelican' and the 'Agnus Dei,' and those at the side the sacred monograms. The white marble mensa is set on a cornice composed of grapevines, and is inlaid with five crosses of red marble. The Super-Altar is of red Lisbon marble, with the words 'HOLY, HOLY, HOLY,' inlaid in mosaics on its face, and its shelf is continued on each side the whole length of the Reredos for the reception of flowers at festivals.

"The design of the Reredos is in the perpendicular style of Gothic, so as to be in keeping with that of the Church. It is constructed of Caen stone, elaborately carved, a great deal of the carving being after natural foliage. In the lower portion on each side of the altar are three square panels filled with colored mosaics in geometrical patterns. Above the line of the Super-Altar are seven panels of white marble, sculptured in alto-relievo, representing incidents in the life of Our Blessed Lord immediately preceding and subsequent to the Last Supper; this is modeled after the celebrated picture by Leonardo da Vinci, and fills the centre panel over the Altar; underneath this appears in raised letters the words, 'Having loved his own which were in the world, he loved them unto the end.' On the right of this panel, under a canopied niche, stands a white marble statuette of St. Raphael with a flaming sword in his hand, and on the left, St. Gabriel, holding a bunch of lilies and a scroll. On the extreme right of the Reredos, in the other panels, are: I. St. Mary Magdalene pouring ointment on the feet of Our Lord, inscribed underneath with the words, 'She hath done what she could'; II. The triumphal entry into Jerusalem, with the words, 'Hosanna to the Son of David'; III. Our Lord washing the disciples' feet, with 'I am among you as he that serveth.' On the left, in continuation, is: IV. The agony in the garden, with the words, 'On Him was laid the iniquity of us all'; V. The betrayal, inscribed with, 'This is your hour and the power of darkness'; and VI. Our Lord before Pilate, who is in the act of saying, 'I find no fault in this man.'

"The Reredos is divided into three bays by buttresses, which contain, under canopies on their face, four doctors of the Church: I. St. Jerome, represented in the act of translating the Bible, accompanied by the Lion endeavoring to show his gratitude for taking the thorn out of his foot; II. St. Ambrose, in bishop's costume, in the attitude of delivering a discourse, with the Beehive, his characteristic emblem, on his left; III. St. Augustine, in same costume as St. Ambrose, in the act of giving the benediction; and IV. St. Gregory, in the act of writing his Homilies. In the centre bay, under a large multifoiled arch, is represented the Crucifixion in high relief. On the right of the Cross stand St. John and St. Mary, the Mother of our Lord; St. Mary Magdalene kneeling embraces the feet which brought such mercy to her; and on the left are the other Mary and the Centurion. This subject is supported on an elaborately carved cornice composed of passion flowers, and underneath are the words, 'Behold the Lamb of God.' Ranged on either side in the two other bays are statuettes of the Twelve Apostles, thirty inches high, each with his characteristic attribute: —

"I. St. Jude carrying a book, and with a club, the weapon with which he was killed.

"II. St. Bartholomew carrying a large knife, the instrument of his martyrdom.

"III. St. Thomas with a builder's rule.

"IV. St. Matthew, who was a tax-gatherer, with a money-box in his left hand, indicative of his calling.

"V. St. John holding a chalice with a serpent issuing from it.

"VI. St. James Minor, first Bishop of Jerusalem, with pen and book, and the fuller's club, the instrument with which he was beaten to death.

"VII. St. Peter with the keys in his right hand and a book in his left.

"VIII. St. Andrew with a transverse cross, similar in shape to that on which he was crucified.

"IX. St. Simon with a saw, the instrument with which he was sawn asunder.

"X. St. Matthias with a book, and an axe to indicate that he was beheaded for his preaching.

"XI. St. Philip holding a tall staff with a Latin cross at the top.

"XII. St. James Major bearing a pilgrim's staff, to which a wallet is suspended, and with a scallop-shell on his flapped hat.

"These statuettes are placed in niches, with traceried heads, carried by polished Bay of Funday red granite shafts, with the background carved in diaper and gilded. On the extreme ends of this line, facing north and south, are the figures of St. Michael and St. George, under canopies similar to those over the Doctors.

"In the centre bay, above the Crucifixion, are sculptured in panels set in diaper work the Resurrection and the Ascension. In the gablet which surmounts it, and inclosed in a Vesica Piscis, is represented Our Lord in his Majesty, holding the globe in his left hand, and blessing with his right; and on either side, and filling the spandrils, are sculptured Angels kneeling in adoration. Underneath the main cornice of the side bays, and forming part of it, is inscribed in raised letters, 'To the Glory of God, in Memory of Wm. B. Astor, this Reredos is erected A.D. 1877.'

"Angels, with uplifted wings, playing on musical instruments (viz.

the Tambourine, the Pandore, the Lyre, and the Cymbals), emblematic of the Church Triumphant, crown the four buttresses.

"The statuary and mosaics were executed in London, and the whole of the carving, Caen stone work of Reredos, and marble work of Altar, including the setting up, was done by Messrs. Ellin and Kitson of this city."

ALTAR AND REREDOS IN TRINITY CHAPEL, NEW YORK CITY

TRINITY CHAPEL, NEW YORK CITY

The lower part of the Reredos against which the Altar is built is of Sienna marble. The design is in the early English Gothic, in keeping with the rest of the building. The upper part is made of Caen stone and is divided into three panels. The figures are of marble, on a background of alabaster. In the centre is the Crucifixion, and on one side, in full relief, St. Mary, and on the other side St. John. The side compartments are subdivided by slender onyx columns into smaller panels with trefoiled heads. On the right of the centre compartment are the figures of St. Peter and St. James the Great and on the left those of St. Andrew and St. Paul. The Altar and Reredos were erected by the congregation of Trinity Chapel in memory of the late Rev. C. E. Swope, D.D. The work was executed by Ellin, Kitson and Co., of New York City, from designs of the architect, Mr. F. C. Withers, of the same city.

CHURCH OF THE TRANSFIGURATION, NEW YORK CITY

The Reredos is constructed of Caen stone, and was erected by Mrs. Zabriskie as a memorial to her mother. It is divided into three parts. On the central one is a representation of Our Lord's Transfiguration. In the side divisions are figures of St. Matthew and St. Luke. Mr. Withers was the architect. The Altar is of white statuary marble and was designed by the Rev. Dr. G. C. Houghton, the Rector of the parish. Borgia Bros. were the builders. A cross and crown form the decoration on the front of the Altar, between the mosaics. On the left the mosaics represent St. Michael in the vestments of a Priest and those on the right St. Gabriel in the vestments of a Deacon. The windows on the side of the Altar were placed by the Altar Society in memory of their first president, Miss Ballow, who held the office for twenty years. Each has the form of an angel carrying a censer, while below are the words, " Holy, Holy, Holy, Lord God of Sabaoth."

ALTAR AND REREDOS IN THE CHURCH OF THE TRANSFIGURATION, NEW YORK CITY

ALTAR AND REREDOS IN THE CHURCH OF ST. IGNATIUS, NEW YORK CITY

CHURCH OF ST. IGNATIUS, NEW YORK CITY

THE Altar is of Vermont statuary marble with Italian marble steps, in white. It was erected in 1886 and the architect was Mr. Kivas Tully, now of St. Louis, Mo. The builders were Fisher and Bird, of New York City. The cost, including the statues, was about $5000. The figures of St. Ignatius and the two others, St. Mary the Virgin and St. Michael, are well executed. The Reredos was enlarged three years ago.

CHURCH OF THE INCARNATION, NEW YORK CITY

WHAT is known as the Constable Chapel was added to the Church in 1903. It was erected to the memory of the late James M. Constable by his children. The Altar and Reredos are constructed of Caen stone. The central representation is that of the Lord's Supper. Figures of the four Evangelists are arranged on each side in canopied niches. The Chancel steps are of marble and the floor mosaic. The words "Wonderful, Counsellor, The Mighty, God, The everlasting Father, The Prince of Peace," are worked in designs in the floor. The architect was Mr. Henry Vaughan, of Boston, and the builders, Evans and Co., of the same city. The cost of the Chapel, Altar, and Reredos was upward of $30,000.

ALTAR AND REREDOS IN THE CONSTABLE CHAPEL IN THE CHURCH OF THE INCARNATION, NEW YORK CITY

ALTAR AND REREDOS IN THE CHURCH OF ST. EDWARD THE MARTYR, NEW YORK CITY

CHURCH OF ST. EDWARD THE MARTYR, NEW YORK CITY

THE Altar is of white marble and was given by Mrs. Harriet B. Ranney in memory of her two sons. It was made and erected by R. Geissler, of New York. The Reredos was added later. It is fifty feet high and twenty feet broad. It is constructed of finely carved oak. The central panel contains a rich mosaic of Christ in Benediction, while the side panels are filled with adoring angels. The richness of the mosaic work in the upper part of the Reredos, the blending of gold and various colors, all present a most pleasing harmony. The Bishop of Fond du Lac writes of the Reredos that " it marks a new stage in the progressive development of ecclesiastical art. The contrast in color between the Choir and the Sanctuary is very effective and significant. The figure of Our Lord vested with outstretched hands, in welcome, not in agony, tell the worshipper of his presence with his people. The details of the work are suggestive and beautiful." The Reredos was executed by J. and R. Lamb, New York City.

CHURCH OF ZION AND ST. TIMOTHY, NEW YORK CITY

The Altar is of white marble and the Reredos of alabaster and Caen stone. They were built in 1891–92. In the niches are five statues. The central one represents Our Blessed Lord and the two on each side the Evangelists. The Altar is eleven and a half feet long and the mensa a solid slab of faultless marble. Between the Altar and Reredos is a narrow Ambulatory to allow the placing of flowers and other ornaments on the Retable. The structure is known as a tomb Altar. The whole is a memorial to the late Rev. George Jarvis Geer, D.D. The architect was Mr. William Halsey Wood and the builder R. Geissler. The cost was about $6000.

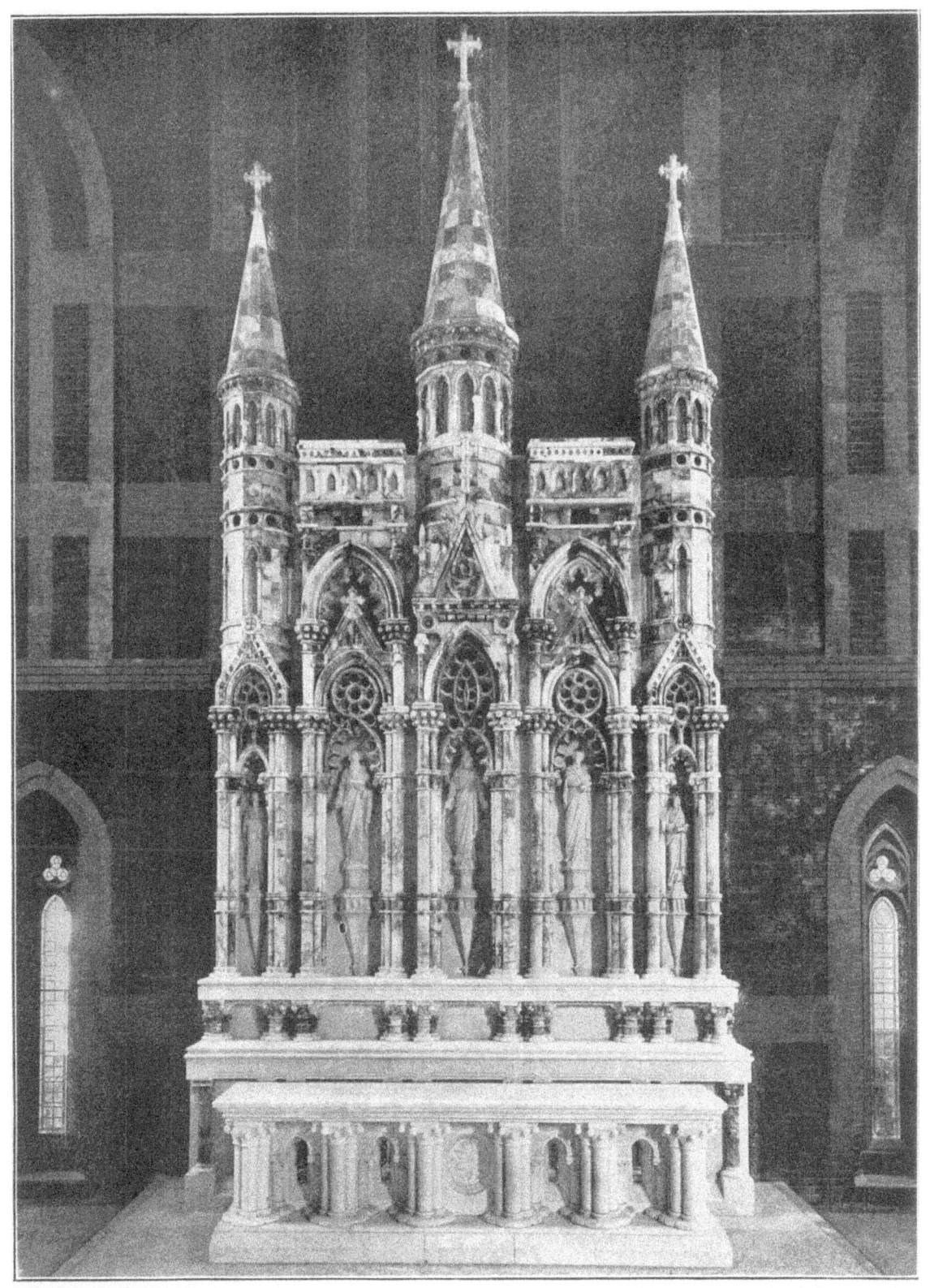
ALTAR AND REREDOS IN THE CHURCH OF ZION AND ST. TIMOTHY, NEW YORK CITY

ALTAR AND REREDOS IN THE CHAPEL OF THE GENERAL THEOLOGICAL SEMINARY, NEW YORK CITY

GENERAL THEOLOGICAL SEMINARY, CHELSEA SQUARE, NEW YORK CITY

THE Altar and Reredos were built in 1888 of English alabaster. The mensa is of white marble and is supported upon pillars of red marble. The Reredos, which is twenty feet wide and sixteen feet high, is constructed with arches supported upon pillars of red marble. The nine niches contain figures of white marble. The central one represents Christ as the Good Shepherd. Those on the Epistle side are St. John the Baptist, St. John, St. Luke, and St. Paul. Those on the Gospel side are Moses, St. Matthew, St. Mark, and St. Peter. The Altar, Reredos, and Rood Screen were the gifts of Mrs. Glorvina R. Hoffman in memory of her husband, Samuel V. Hoffman. These persons were the parents of the late Dean Hoffman. The architect was Mr. Charles C. Haight and the builder Mr. R. C. Fisher, both of New York City. The cost of the Altar and Reredos without the statuary was $5975.

ST. JAMES' CHURCH, PHILADELPHIA, PA.

The Altar and Reredos were the gifts of Mrs. Howard J. Gibson, in memory of her deceased husband. The material used is Caen stone for the Reredos and Iowa marble for the Altar. There are twenty-eight statues of stone, the principal and larger ones being arranged in a row of ten. The subjects of these, going from left to right, are as follows: 1. St. Columba; 2. St. Edward the Martyr; 3. St. Thomas of Canterbury; 4. St. John the Baptist; 5. The Blessed Virgin Mary; 6. St. John; 7. Isaiah; 8. Aaron; 9. David; 10. Moses. The Sedilia and Credence are of stone built up solidly from the floor. The designers were Cram, Goodhue, and Ferguson, and the builders were J. F. Whitman and Co., of Philadelphia.

ALTAR AND REREDOS IN THE CHURCH OF ST. JAMES, PHILADELPHIA, PA.

ALTAR AND REREDOS IN ST. STEPHEN'S CHURCH, PHILADELPHIA, PA.

ST. STEPHEN'S CHURCH, PHILADELPHIA, PA.

THE Reredos was unveiled on January 17, 1889. It was erected by Mrs. James Magee in memory of her mother. The Last Supper fills the central part and was designed by Salviati. The workmen of this artist executed the work under the direction of Mr. Henry Holiday, of London. In a letter of July 6, 1888, the latter writes: "Your mosaic is at length completed. It was on view last Saturday and Sunday. I ought to say that Mrs. Holiday, who has great experience in embroidery, an art closely allied in spirit to mosaic, has assisted me in the execution of the work. All the heads have been executed by Mrs. Holiday and myself." The mosaic measures twelve by five feet. It is said to contain upwards of 180,000 pieces.

ST. ELIZABETH'S CHURCH, PHILADELPHIA

The following description appeared in *The Living Church* for August 11, 1906:—

"A magnificent altar was dedicated on the Eighth Sunday after Trinity at St. Elizabeth's Church by the Rt. Rev. William Walter Webb, D.D., Bishop Coadjutor of Milwaukee, who was the second Rector of the parish, succeeding the late Rev. Henry Robert Percival, D.D., the founder of the parish. The Altar and Reredos are in 'English-Italian' and 'American Pavanazia' marbles, with carver caps and ornaments in Caen stone, gilded. The tabernacle is of white Alabama marble with gilded ornaments and the door is of bronze, made in Paris, gilded, and contains precious stones, and a Latin cross with *Agnus Dei* in centre. The subject of the large painting in the Reredos is 'The Resurrection and the Four Evangelists,' copied especially for St. Elizabeth's Church, by Eugenio Capelli, of Florence, who has painted a number of other pictures for this Church. The original of the Altarpiece is in the Pitti Gallery, Florence, by Fra Bartolomeo. The inscription on the pediment is *D. O. M. sub Invocatione S. Elizabeth.* The first design for the Altar was drawn by the Rev. W. H. McClellan, one of the priests connected with St. Elizabeth's, and Messrs. Bailey and Bassett were the supervising architects. The marble work was done by Sharpless and Watts. Some five hundred members and friends of the parish contributed toward this Altar, many of its parts being special memorial gifts. The pilasters and gradines were given by the Sunday Schools of the parish, who have raised over $600 for the same during the past year. The total cost is $2600."

ALTAR AND REREDOS IN ST. ELIZABETH'S CHURCH, PHILADELPHIA, PA.

ALTAR AND REREDOS IN THE CHURCH OF THE SAVIOUR, WEST PHILADELPHIA, PA.

CHURCH OF THE SAVIOUR, WEST PHILADELPHIA

BACK of the Altar there is a marble elevation with the Agnus Dei at the top and on the slab are the words "Blessing and honor and glory and power, be unto him that sitteth upon the throne and unto the Lamb for ever and ever."

The mural decorations, by Mr. Edwin H. Blashfield, are memorials to the late Anthony J. Drexel, a prominent banker and philanthropist and the founder of the Drexel Institute of Philadelphia. He was also the Senior Warden of the Parish.

Of the decorations the art editor of *The Public Ledger* thus writes: —

"The scheme of the composition presents a choir of angels surrounding a figure which holds the Grail. The color scheme ultimately resolves itself into a burst of golden light, although blues predominate amidst a related mass of pale tints, the latter serving to modulate the color into rich harmony. Gold has been freely used everywhere. The flat massing of the halos and the simple treatment of the figures suggest the old masters studied by the pre-Raphaelite school, Mr. Blashfield's treatment being thoroughly modern, however. What the old art has to teach is here assimilated and made part of an art new and beautiful and strong.

"The planets in nebulous spots of gold and the cloud masses, although hazily suggested in the composition with amazing skill, considering the difficulty of the heavy color, are brilliantly handled so as to suggest the idea of being in some place that is other-worldly. The idea and the means are trite, but the artist's treatment is such that the philosophical concept of the whole design becomes an inseparable part of the execution. In this it recalls the Sargent decoration in the Boston Library and the Velasquez 'Coronation of the Virgin' in Madrid.

"The decoration is brilliant rather than calm. Yet even this vibrant quality contrives to carry the eye, and the mind, too, direct to the central figure, which is of great beauty and dignity. Here the gold is touched into a vivid flame of scarlet, this being the highest note in the composition, toward which all leads and from which all modulates.

"The lower wall behind the Altar presents conventionalized figures, eleven in number, presenting various types of humanity. Gold is here used again, but in subordination, on the thin line of the halos and the embossed embroidery of the rich draperies. The decorative use of the unopened bud of the lily is brought into the composition effectively and with something of novelty."

ALTAR AND REREDOS IN ST. MARY'S CHURCH, WEST PHILADELPHIA, PA.

ST. MARY'S CHURCH, WEST PHILADELPHIA, PA.

The Altar and Reredos are fine examples of modern mosaic work made in the studios of Rome. The marble sculpture is by Valenzi, the Byzantine mosaic by Leonardi, and the Roman mosaic by Rubicondi, each famous in his line. The marble forming the framework of the pictures is twenty-two feet eight inches in height by ten feet eight inches in breadth. In the apex of the Gothic Reredos is a representation of the Ascension. Below this in the great central panel is a mosaic of the Crucifixion after Guido Reni. On a broad panel nearly the whole width of the Retable is the Nativity, with the adoration of the wise men and the shepherds. The smaller panels are symbolical. Those on the left contain the emblems of the Passion and those on the right the symbols of the Eucharist. Many of the stones in the panels were gathered in Palestine, Syria, Egypt, and the East. The twisted columns are also inlaid with colored stones in Byzantine style. The face of the Altar has the Agnus Dei, flanked by Alpha and Omega. The Altar was built under the direction of the Rev. J. Bloomfield Wetherill as a memorial to his mother, Mrs. Isabella Macomb Wetherill, widow of Dr. William Wetherill, who died on Christmas Day, 1871. The Altar was exhibited in the Italian art department at the Centennial Exposition in Philadelphia in 1876. After the death of Rev. Mr. Wetherill in 1886 it was made a memorial of him as well as of his mother, and the ends of the Altar bear inscriptions to this effect. It was presented to St. Mary's parish by Mr. William H. Wetherill, the letter of the Vestry accepting the gift bearing date of January 22, 1890. The original cost of the Altar, aside from its transportation and putting in place, was $25,000.

ST. TIMOTHY'S CHURCH, ROXBOROUGH, PHILADELPHIA, PA.

The Altar was erected in 1893 of pink African marble. It has two gradines of colored French marble. The central panel of the Reredos is made of vitreous mosaic, the workmanship of Hardman and Sons, of London. It represents the Lord in glory, crowned, and holding a globe, while surrounded by angels, swinging censers. In the wing of the Reredos, on the left side as you face the Altar, are Moses, Aaron, Noah, David, and St. John the Baptist. The wing on the other side contains five of the Apostles. All these figures are in the attitude of adoration looking toward the glorified Christ. The two wings were constructed as a memorial to Mary Sophia Merrick and were erected in 1898 at the cost of $1500. The total cost of the whole work was $3500. The marble builders were Atkinson and Mylhertz, and the architects, G. W. and W. D. Hewitt, of Philadelphia.

ALTAR AND REREDOS IN ST. TIMOTHY'S CHURCH, ROXBOROUGH, PHILADELPHIA

ALTAR AND REREDOS IN ST. LUKE'S CHURCH, GERMANTOWN, PA.

ST. LUKE'S CHURCH, GERMANTOWN, PA.

The Altar and Reredos were erected in 1903, and dedicated on the eve of Whitsunday of that year. The material used in construction is Caen stone. The architect was Mr. George T. Pearson, of Philadelphia, and the builders were J. P. Whitman Co. of the same city. The middle of the Reredos represents the Crucifixion, and the niches on each side will in time be filled with Scripture characters. This beautiful work of art is a memorial of the late William Penn Troth, Jr.

ST. PETER'S CHURCH, GERMANTOWN, PA.

The Altar and Reredos were erected in 1896. The material used is Caen stone. There are six carved figures. Looking east toward the Altar, on the extreme left is St. Peter and on the extreme right, St. Paul. Between these are St. Matthew, St. Mark, St. Luke, and St. John. The architect was Theophilus P. Chandler, of Philadelphia, and the builder, William J. Gruhler, of Germantown. The cost was $2500. The work is a memorial to Henry Howard Houston, by his widow. The beauty of the Altar and Reredos are much enhanced by the artistic surroundings of the Chancel and Sanctuary.

ALTAR AND REREDOS IN ST. PETER'S CHURCH, GERMANTOWN, PA.

ALTAR AND REREDOS IN GRACE CHURCH, BALTIMORE, MD.

GRACE CHURCH, BALTIMORE, MD.

ERECTED in 1898. The architect was Henry M. Congdon. The main subject of the Reredos is the Institution of the Lord's Supper. The side figures represent St. John the Baptist and St. Luke. The subjects in bas-relief on the Altar front are Sacrifice of Noah, Melchizedek, and Abraham, and Sacrifice of Isaac. The cost was $9000. It was erected by Mrs. William M. Innez to the memory of her husband and children.

CHURCH OF THE EPIPHANY, WASHINGTON, D.C.

The Reredos was erected in 1902 and is constructed of Indiana limestone. The architecture is Gothic. The central representation is the Institution of the Lord's Supper carved in high relief. A sculptured angel is placed in a niche on each side of the Altar. An elaborate canopy gives beauty and effectiveness to the whole structure. The Reredos was the work of Mr. Henry Randall, architect, and Mr. W. O. Partridge, sculptor.

ALTAR AND REREDOS IN THE CHURCH OF THE EPIPHANY, WASHINGTON, D.C.

ALTAR AND REREDOS IN ST. PAUL'S CHURCH, WASHINGTON, D.C.

ST. PAUL'S CHURCH, WASHINGTON, D.C.

THE Reredos was erected during the summer of 1898 and is constructed of Caen stone and Tennessee marble. The pillars of the arches in which stand the statuettes and also the pillars of the Altar supporting the mensa are of alabaster. In the Reredos are figures of the four Evangelists, and at each end larger figures of St. Peter and St. Paul. The passion vine adorns the central arch, and on the Tabernacle are panels of grapes and wheat. The Reredos is a memorial of Mrs. Henry Harding Carter, a benefactress of the parish. The architect and builder was Mr. R. Geissler of New York City. The Altar is a general memorial of departed communicants. The cost of the Altar was about $1200, and of the Reredos $1700.

EMMANUEL CHURCH, BOSTON, MASS.

The Altar and Reredos were erected in the summer of 1899. The material used is Caen stone, which against the soft gray of the Indiana limestone forming the walls of the apse is extremely effective. In the central canopy is the figure of Our Lord, with hands outstretched. In the side canopies are adoring angels in a kneeling attitude. The bas-relief below represents the Lord's Supper. As we face it the canopied figures on the right are St. Mary and St. John and those on the left St. Peter and St. Martha. Directly over the Altar are two small angels bearing a scroll with the words, "Holy, Holy, Holy, Lord God Almighty." The Altar and Reredos were given by Mrs. Winthrop Sargent as a memorial to her father and mother, Mr. and Mrs. Benjamin P. Rotch, and their son and daughter. This work of art was designed by Mr. Francis R. Allen of Boston and the erection completed by John Evans and Co., also of Boston. Mr. Mora, an artist in their employ, modeled the figures. The cost of the Altar and Reredos was $10,000.

ALTAR AND REREDOS IN EMMANUEL CHURCH, BOSTON, MASS.

ALTAR AND REREDOS IN THE CHURCH OF THE ADVENT, BOSTON, MASS.

CHURCH OF THE ADVENT, BOSTON, MASS.

THE High Altar, with the lower portion of the Reredos, including the Crucifixion, was designed by Mr. John H. Sturgis, the architect of the Church. The upper part of the Reredos, with the open tracery, was designed by Mr. Harold Peto, of London. The Altar and Reredos were put in at different times and were the gifts of Mrs. Gardner in memory of her husband, Mr. John Lowell Gardner.

ALL SAINTS' CHURCH, DORCHESTER, MASS.

The Reredos was erected in 1898 of Caen stone. It was designed by Cram, Goodhue, and Ferguson and executed by John Evans and Co., of Boston. The central statue is Our Lord, blessing his Church, and holding the orb of dominion. On the right of Christ is St. Michael the Archangel and on the left is St. Gabriel. The smaller figures represent a scheme of Church history, Jewish and Christian. They are Aaron, St. John the Baptist, David, St. Clement, St. Peter, St. Athanasius, St. Stephen, St. John the Evangelist, St. James the Less, St. Alban, St. Paul, and St. Columba. The designer and sculptor of the figures was Mr. Mora. The cost of the Altar and Reredos was $11,000. They are in memory of Colonel Oliver White Peabody.

ALTAR AND REREDOS IN ALL SAINTS' CHURCH, DORCHESTER, MASS.

ALTAR AND REREDOS IN CHRIST CHURCH, NEW HAVEN, CONN.

CHRIST CHURCH, NEW HAVEN, CONN.

THE Altar and Reredos were completed in time for Christmas Day, 1906, and consecrated at a special service on the first Sunday after Epiphany, January 13, 1907. The Altar is constructed of Knoxville marble and the Reredos of Caen stone. The central subject that stands out prominently is the Crucifixion. It is admirably executed and most attractive. The face of Our Lord is expressive of the peacefulness of death combined with the confidence and majesty of one who has conquered. On either side of the cross are the figures of the Virgin Mother and St. John. At the foot of the cross is a pelican nourishing her young with her own blood, symbolizing Christ giving his life for his children. Below this, under a canopy, is depicted the Nativity, with St. Mary and St. Joseph adoring the holy Child. The four figures on the sides of the Nativity are St. John the Baptist, St. Stephen, St. Anne, and St. Elizabeth. In the niches at the top of the cross are the four angels, St. Michael, St. Uriel, St. Raphael, and St. Gabriel. The large niches on the sides of the Reredos contain statues of St. Athanasius, St. John Chrysostom, St. Augustine, and St. Ambrose. The large figures in the niches in the wall are St. Peter and St. Paul. On the front of the Altar is a relief of the Entombment. On either side are angels bearing scrolls. The architect of the work was Mr. Henry Vaughan, of Boston, and the builders John Evans and Co., of the same city. This artistic work was not a memorial but the generous gift of Mrs. Mary E. Ives, who made it, as she says, "expressive of the honor and glory of the risen Lord."

CHURCH OF THE HOLY TRINITY, MIDDLETOWN, CONN.

The Altar was erected in 1890 by Coxe Sons and Vining of New York City. It is the gift of Mrs. Hugh T. Dickey, formerly of Chicago, and a sister of the late Rev. James De Koven, D.D., of Racine. It is in memory of her two sons. The Reredos is the gift of the same donor in memory of Judge Dickey, her husband. It is of Caen stone with panels of white marble carved to illustrate Moses and Elias on each side of the central panel of the Crucifixion. It was erected in 1894. Mr. J. M. Rhind of New York was the sculptor, and Mr. Haight of the same city, the architect.

ALTAR AND REREDOS IN THE CHURCH OF THE HOLY TRINITY, MIDDLETOWN, CONN.

ALTAR AND REREDOS IN GRACE CHURCH, WINDSOR, CONN.

GRACE CHURCH, WINDSOR, CONN.

The Altar and Reredos were erected in January, 1907, and blessed by Bishop Brewer, January 31. The material is white Carrara marble, slightly veined, relieved by small columns and panels of yellow Siena marble, with considerable dark veining. The three picture panels represent the Conversion of Cornelius, the first army officer to enter the Church, for the whole is a memorial to the late Colonel John Mason Loomis, of Chicago, who raised and commanded the Twenty-sixth Illinois Volunteer Infantry during the Civil War. On the left is seen the Roman Captain kneeling, with the angel standing over him. Below are the words: "Thy prayers and thine alms are come up for a memorial before God." On the right Cornelius sits and St. Peter stands, proclaiming: "He that feareth God and worketh righteousness is accepted with him." The mosaics were suggested by the Rector of the parish, the Rev. Dr. Harriman. They are as follows: In the centre Christ with Cleopas and the other disciple at the Supper at Emmaus. Inscribed below are these words in gilt letters: "He was known of them in breaking of bread." The side pictures above are of glass mosaic, made in London by Heaton, Butler, and Bayne. The pavement of small mosaic blocks and the carved steps are of gray Knoxville, Tennessee, marble. All the work was done by the Gorham Co. of New York City, and their designer Mr. Schweichart made the whole plan. The cost of the work was a little over $4000.

ST. JOHN'S CHURCH, STAMFORD, CONN.

The Altar and Reredos were erected in 1890. The material used is Caen stone. The lower panels of the Reredos represent the Agony in the Garden and the Entombment of Christ. The upper panels portray the Crucifixion and the Resurrection. The central compartment indicates the Last Supper. Angels and Evangelists are in the niches. The sculptor was James Smith, the architect, William A. Potter, and Norcross Bros. the builders.

ALTAR AND REREDOS IN ST. JOHN'S CHURCH, STAMFORD, CONN.

ALTAR AND REREDOS IN TRINITY CHURCH, TORRINGTON, CONN.

TRINITY CHURCH, TORRINGTON, CONN.

The Altar is constructed of Caen stone, ornamented with polished marbles and inlaid work. It is nine feet long and two and one-half deep. The Reredos is of the same stone and has upon the riser of the Retable the words: " Behold, O God, our defender, and look upon the face of thine anointed." In the central niche is the figure of Our Lord in the attitude of invitation. On either side stand St. Mary and St. John, flanked at either end by St. Gabriel, bearing the lily of the annunciation and St. Michael with the sword of the warrior. These are in niches with detached and separating shafts of polished marbles of varying colors, while the background is of golden Siena marble. The upper part of the Reredos in gabled canopies and carved work is surmounted by carved cornices and battlemented cresting, flanked by turrets, and showing a floriated cross in the centre. The width of the Reredos is ten feet and the height from the Sanctuary floor to the top of the central cross is sixteen feet. As a fitting suggestion of the service of the Altar, above it are painted on the wall kneeling angels in robes of white and swinging golden censers. The architect was Mr. Henry M. Congdon of New York and the builders Peter Theis' Sons.

CHAPEL OF ST. PAUL'S SCHOOL, CONCORD, N.H.

ERECTED in 1894. The architect was Henry Vaughan, and the builders were Irving and Casson, of Boston. The paintings were done by Clayton and Bell, of London. The large painting directly over the Altar represents the Adoration of the Magi. The four smaller ones on the side give scenes in the Nativity of Christ. The large pictures to the right and left indicate the Annunciation to the Virgin Mary and the Baptism of Our Lord. The two pictures in the second row are the Transfiguration and Resurrection of Christ. The carved figure under the central spire of the Reredos is a seated statue of Christ with his left hand resting on a globe and his right hand raised in benediction. To his right and left arranged in niches are six fathers of the Church. Six smaller figures are arranged about the Reredos, who represent angels bearing shields having on them the emblems of the Passion. The Altar is of Tennessee marble and is a memorial of Mrs. Richard Conover, of South Amboy. It cost $1000. The Reredos is of oak and is a memorial to the eldest son of Mr. Cornelius Vanderbilt and was erected at a cost of $15,000.

ALTAR AND REREDOS IN THE CHAPEL OF ST. PAUL'S SCHOOL, CONCORD, N.H.

ALTAR AND REREDOS IN ST. STEPHEN'S CHURCH, PROVIDENCE, R.I.

ST. STEPHEN'S CHURCH, PROVIDENCE, R.I.

This large Reredos is about twenty feet high and is divided into seventeen compartments filled with a series of paintings. Around the whole is a carved framework of pierced foliage, with projecting wings on either side of open tracery. The Altar and Reredos were consecrated on St. Stephen's Day, 1883, by the Bishop of the Diocese. The sermon was preached by the Rev. Lucius Waterman, D.D., at that time a professor in the Seabury Divinity School at Faribault, Minn. This work of art was erected in honor of a former Rector, as the following inscription shows: —

"This Altar and Reredos
are consecrated to
the greater glory of
GOD
in grateful remembrance of
HENRY WATERMAN,
Priest and Doctor,
who, by the grace given him,
restored to the Church in Providence
some forfeited treasures of primitive piety,
notably,
the Daily Service in the Season of Lent,
and
the Weekly Celebration of the
HOLY EUCHARIST.
It was given him also
to teach
to some penitents the joy of Absolution
and
to some mourners the comfort of prayer
for the faithful dead.
In such works
of restoration,
which could not but trouble some quiet hearts,
he himself was called to endure grief deeply,
to the shortening of his days
for JESUS' sake.
Think upon him, my GOD, for good
according to all that he hath done
for this people."

Nine years later the work was completed by filling the panels with paintings. The artist of these designs and of the Tabernacle was Mr. Roger Watts of the firm of John Hardman and Co., London. The subjects of the paintings follow a carefully prepared plan as indicated in the words of another, who says: "The whole scheme is governed by the principle of ancient English Church symbolism, that the Chancel, being emblematic of the Church triumphant, should portray only scenes of life and joy. The Rood Screen is the gate of death, and so there should be depicted the Crucifixion. With this idea, the large central panel of the Reredos, dominating the entire work, represents Jesus Christ in glory, enthroned as King of Kings and Lord of Lords. He wears a splendid crown, from which rays of glory stream, forming a cross. He holds the orb and cross, the sceptre of the world. On his breast shine the letters Alpha and Omega. His throne is supported by four archangels, proclaiming to the four quarters of the universe his praise, as they hear the legend: 'Holy Holy, Holy, Lord God of Sabaoth.' Around his throne bends the rainbow. Surrounding him is a rosy circle of angel faces — the seraphs, on fire with love. Another outer circle of angels with azure wings are the cherubs.

"On the Epistle side of this picture is the Adoration of the Magi, to teach us of the Nativity and of Christ's Manifestation to the Gentiles. On the Gospel side is the Annunciation, to set forth the fact of the Incarnation, 'conceived of the Holy Ghost.'

"In the central panel of the next lower tier are the Madonna and Child. Around the Virgin's Throne are placed four figures representing Old Testament types of Mary, the second Eve. These are Eve, Judith, Esther, and Rachel. On the Epistle side of the Virgin are St. Paul, closely associated with the introduction of Christianity into Britain, and whose conversion has always been believed by holy men to have been an answer to St. Stephen's dying prayer for his murderers; then St. Athanasius, as a great champion of the Catholic faith, treading under his feet a scroll marked Arians, and then St. Chrysostom, as representing the Greek Church, and whose name is so familiar to Anglicans from the prayer ascribed to him in the Daily Offices.

"On the Gospel side of the Blessed Virgin is St. Stephen, the name saint of the Church, next to him St. Alban, the first British martyr, and then St. Ambrose, as representing the Latin Church, and whose name has always been traditionally associated with the Te Deum. The row of pictures nearest the Altar is designed to teach the Resurrection. The front of the Tabernacle (made in London, of elaborately carved oak, richly gilded) is supposed to be the door of the Sepulchre. Here is a lovely figure of the Angel of the Resurrection seated on the stone. From the Epistle side approach the three Marys, Mary Magdalene, Mary, the wife of Cleophas, and Mary Salome, with their boxes of sweet spices, while on the Gospel side are St. John, St. Peter, and St. James."

The final additions took the form of a separate memorial, as expressed in the following inscription: —

"The Tabernacle
and
The Paintings of the Reredos
are consecrated
to the greater Glory of GOD
and in loving memory
of
Lyman Klapp,
sometime Vestryman of this Church
who entered into Rest
Sept. 27th, A. D. 1889.
Requiescat in pace."

The architect of the Altar and Reredos was Mr. Henry Vaughan, of Boston. The painted panels after their execution in London were put in position by Irving and Casson, also of Boston. The carving of the Reredos was executed by Evans and Tombs.

ST. PAUL'S CHURCH, CHATTANOOGA, TENN.

The Altar and Reredos were erected in 1886 at the completion of the Church. The architect was William Halsey Wood, and the builders the Endolithic Marble Co., of New York City. The central figure is that of Christ with outstretched arms in an attitude of welcome. The side panels represent adoring angels. The figures are painted and burned according to the Endolithic process. The Altar and Reredos are in memory of William Wadley Yonge, who was a vestryman at the time of his death in 1885. The cost was $1800.

ALTAR AND REREDOS IN ST. PAUL'S CHURCH, CHATTANOOGA, TENN.

ALTAR AND REREDOS IN THE CHURCH OF ST. MICHAEL AND ALL ANGELS, ANNISTON, ALA.

CHURCH OF ST. MICHAEL AND ALL ANGELS, ANNISTON, ALA.

THE Altar and Reredos were consecrated on St. Michael's and All Angels' Day, 1888. The Altar is of Italian marble and is twelve feet six inches long by two feet six inches wide. The Reredos from floor to pinnacles is built of English alabaster. In the central niche is a figure of St. Michael five feet high. On the right is St. Gabriel and on the left St. Raphael. These two latter figures are four feet six inches high. Seven figures, also of alabaster, crown the pinnacles. These are four feet high. The architect was Mr. William Halsey Wood, and the builders, Stewart and Hendry, of Newark, N.J. The whole Church, including the Altar and Reredos, was the splendid gift of John W. Noble, Esq., of Anniston, the whole being a memorial of his father and brother. The cost of the Altar and Reredos was $10,000.

ST. LUKE'S CHURCH, SCRANTON, PA.

The Altar and Reredos were completed for Easter Day, 1905. The architect was Mr. Tiffany, of New York, and the builders, the Whitman Co., of Philadelphia. The Altar is built of white statuary marble, and the Reredos of Caen stone. The front of the Altar has three panels, the central one representing the Ark of the Covenant, with the outstretched wings of the cherubim covering the mercy-seat. This is a reproduction of M. Tissot's picture. On each side panel is an adoring angel with upturned face. The Reredos has also three panels with figures in half relief. The middle one represents the Crucifixion with a grouping of St. Mary, St. Joseph, and St. Mary Magdalene. The left panel facing the east represents Melchizedek bringing forth bread and wine and blessing Abraham, pointing to that " pure offering " which prophecy declared should be offered to the Most High. The right panel contains a representation of the Supper at Emmaus, where Our Lord made himself known to the disciples in the breaking of bread. These panels also are reproductions of the pictures of Tissot. This artistic work was erected by the Jermyn family as a memorial to the late John Jermyn, who was Warden of the parish from 1887 to 1889.

ALTAR AND REREDOS IN ST. LUKE'S CHURCH, SCRANTON, PA.

ALTAR AND REREDOS IN TRINITY CHURCH, GENEVA, N.Y.

TRINITY CHURCH, GENEVA, N.Y.

The Altar and Reredos were erected in 1906 and consecrated on All Saints' Day. The material used is Caen stone. The figures on either side are St. Gabriel and St. Michael. The architect was George T. Pearson, of Philadelphia. The sculptors and builders were the J. Franklin Whitman Co. The Reredos is a memorial to Bishop Coxe and the Altar to Mr. and Mrs. A. M. Patterson. The cost was $5250.

CHAPEL OF THE CONVENT OF ST. MARY, PEEKSKILL, N.Y.

The Altar and Reredos were erected in 1893 of various kinds of marble. The central statue represents the Virgin Mary and the Holy Child. On the south side in niches are: 1. St. Michael; 2. Angel of the Passion, with instruments of the Passion; 3. Angel of Praise with Censer. On the north side are: 1. St. Gabriel; 2. Angel of the Passion; 3. Angel of Praise. The architect was Henry M. Congdon, of New York. The sculptor was Joseph Sibbel. The cost was about $7000.

ALTAR AND REREDOS IN THE CHAPEL OF THE CONVENT OF ST. MARY, PEEKSKILL, N.Y.

ALTAR IN THE CHURCH OF THE ASCENSION, CHICAGO, ILL.

CHURCH OF THE ASCENSION, CHICAGO, ILL.

The present High Altar of the Church of the Ascension, Chicago, was erected in 1893. It is the gift of Mrs. Alice Lord Wheeler, since deceased, and was placed in the Church as a memorial of her father, Mr. Gilderoy Lord, of Watertown, N.Y. The Altar was designed by Edward J. N. Stent, of New York. Vermont statuary marble was used in its construction, the mensa being a single slab of eleven feet in length. For the more delicate carving, such as the capitals of the pillars and the ornamentation of the canopy, Carrara marble was used. The pillars themselves are of Mexican onyx. The two angels are of alabaster and were made in Southwark, London. The mosaics of the Tabernacle door, and of the panels in the face of the Altar, are from the works of Salviati in Venice.

CHAPEL OF THE CONVENT OF THE NATIVITY, FOND DU LAC, WIS.

The Altar and Reredos were erected in 1906, and are constructed of quartered white oak. In the Reredos are five carved figures. The central one is that of Christ in the attitude of the Teacher. On his one hand are St. Hilda and St. Mary the Penitent, and on the other, St. Catherine of Siena and St. Martha. The cost was $3000. The designers and builders were the American Seating Co., of Manitowoc, Wis.

ALTAR AND REREDOS IN THE CONVENT OF THE NATIVITY, FOND DU LAC, WIS.

ALTAR AND REREDOS IN ST. MARY'S CHURCH, KANSAS CITY, MO.

ST. MARY'S CHURCH, KANSAS CITY, MO.

The Altar and Reredos were erected in 1887 of white marble richly colored. The decoration is known as Endolithic work. The stone is heated and the colors applied, which sink in, for the most part, through the whole thickness. It is a patent process, not now on the market. The four-figures in the Reredos represent St. John the Evangelist and St. Anna on the Epistle side and St. Joseph and St. Elizabeth on the Gospel side. This work of art is a memorial to the Rev. Henry David Jardine, who was for some time the Rector of the parish. He died January 10, 1886.

The following inscriptions are on the Altar: —

On the base of the Reredos: "BENEDICTUS FRUCTUS VENTRIS TUI."

Above the panel: "BENEDICTA TU IN MULIERIBUS."

On the base of the Altar: "IN HONOREM BEATA MARIAE VIRGINIS: AD GLORIAM DEI: IN MEMORIAM HENRICA DAVIDIS, SACERDOTIS."

The design of the door of the Tabernacle of the Altar is taken from the Catacomb of St. Pontineus at Rome. It represents a jeweled cross beautified with a rose of Sharon on each side.

The following description is given by Caryl Coleman, the designer of the Altar: —

"The central panel of the Altar is intended to illustrate the text of Scripture, 'Blessed art thou among women.' The Holy Mother is the central figure, enthroned as the queen of womanhood, and holding upon her knees her Divine Son, through whom she has a right to her position in the scheme of Christ's redemption. On her right, kneeling, is the virgin martyr, St. Agnes. Behind her, St. Theresa (who, although a woman, holds the rank of a Doctor in the Church), a virgin, a religious, and a reformer. At her side and upon her knees is the figure of St. Catherine of Siena, one whose life carried out the combined qualities displayed in the lives of Martha and Mary. Behind her, and standing up, is the figure of St. Mary Magdalene de Pazzi, a recluse and contemplative. On the left of the Blessed Virgin, and kneeling at her feet, worshiping her Divine Son, is represented the chief of penitents, St. Mary Magdalene. Behind her and standing, the figure of St. Bridget of Sweden, a saintly and holy widow, whose prayers reached the highest point of union with God. At her side and upon her knees, St. Elizabeth of Hungary, the saint who has a right to three crowns, as she represented three lives, the virgin, the wife, and the widow. Behind her and standing up, with head bowed, in all humility, that most wonderful of all penitents, St. Margaret of Cortona. The background is composed of flowers, symbolical of the various states of life represented in the panel. The idea was to gather in this panel women of every nation, to show the broadness of Catholicity, and that all women were to choose the Holy Mother as their model. As we go over the names we note a Hebrew, a Roman, a Spaniard, a Swede, a German, and an Italian. All the personages represented are treated in their proper religious habits and symbolic colors; St. Theresa is habited in the Carmelite costume, St. Margaret of Cortona in the Franciscan, St. Bridget of Sweden in the habit of the order of Sion, while St. Elizabeth of Hungary is in her princely garb. Those who were married are without the virgin's wreath but wear the marriage veil; St. Mary Magdalene, neither crowned nor veiled, is yet, as she always appears to us in Holy Scripture, at the feet of Jesus."

ALTAR AND REREDOS IN GRACE CHURCH, UTICA, NEW YORK

GRACE CHURCH, UTICA, N.Y.

The Chancel was rebuilt and enlarged about the year 1890. The younger Upjohn of New York was the architect, as his father had been the original architect of the whole church. The late John F. Hughes, of Utica, was the contractor.

The exterior of the Chancel, like the Church, is of gray sandstone with white limestone trimmings. The window trimmings, tracery, and large chancel arch, also the niched wainscot inside, are of Indiana limestone. There is a barrel-vaulted ceiling of Georgia pine.

The ends of the roof beams are carved singing angels, the corbels of the Chancel arch are praying angels, the capitals of the columns represent different sorts of foliage. The panels of the stone wainscot are incised with a conventional diapering of different designs.

The Reredos and Altar are of Caen stone. The conventional work, designed by Upjohn, was executed by Karl Bitter. The large central panel represents the Ascension, after the idea of Doré's painting of the same subject.

The whole Chancel, including Altar, windows, and Reredos, was designed to be a memorial to Alfred and Elizabeth Munson, Samuel Alfred Munson, and James Watson Williams, the parents, brother, and husband of Helen Elizabeth Munson Williams. As her death occurred during the progress of the work, her daughters agreed to build it and join their mother's name with the others commemorated.

The six mosaic panels were made by Pellarin, of New York, the mosaic being made on purpose for the designs, in Italy. They represent on each side furthest from the Altar the Rose of Sharon, the next two panels represent the Passion Flower, and the two nearest the Altar represent the Vine. They also are a memorial to Helen Elizabeth Munson Williams, and to all those in the church not otherwise remembered.

ST. JOHN'S AMERICAN EPISCOPAL CHURCH, DRESDEN, GERMANY

This Church was erected and beautified chiefly by the American residents of Dresden. The Altar, Font, and Pulpit were the gifts of Mrs. J. E. Thompson, of St. Paul, Minn., and were given in memory of her husband, while she was a resident of Dresden. All the marble work is of the finest Italian quality. The front of the Altar represents the Last Supper, and is a work of art. The chief decoration of the Reredos is a Crucifixion scene finely executed in marble. The three gifts footed up the sum of $7000.

ALTAR AND REREDOS IN ST. JOHN'S AMERICAN CHURCH, DRESDEN, GERMANY

SILVER ALTAR IN THE LADY CHAPEL OF ST. MARK'S CHURCH, PHILADELPHIA, PA.

SILVER ALTAR IN THE LADY CHAPEL OF ST. MARK'S CHURCH, PHILADELPHIA, PA.

THE following description is taken from a pamphlet bearing the imprint of Barkentin and Krall, Regent Street, London: "Visitors to Florence will recall, amongst the treasures of that great treasury of all the arts, the superb silver Altar which is now exhibited in the Museum of the Cathedral, and which is, or rather was, carried year by year to the Baptistery of the Cathedral, to be used on the Feast of St. John the Baptist. Since Ant. Pallajuolo (1429–98) and his brother artists designed and made that celebrated Altar, nothing, so far as we know, has been produced at all approaching it in elaborate magnificence, until the present time, when Mr. Krall, and the artists and craftsmen associated with him, have made the Altar for the Lady Chapel of St. Mark's, Philadelphia. It will add to the interest of those who visit St. Mark's, as well as of those who are accustomed to worship there, to have at hand some description of the construction, the arrangement, and iconography of this very splendid piece of modern ecclesiastical art.

"The Altar, seven feet in length by two feet in depth, and three feet three inches in height, consists of a mensa or slab, in one piece of gray and black Irish marble, supported on a frame of solid silver, backed by wood. The original idea was to provide simply a movable frontal to the existing alabaster Altar, to be used only on Feasts of Our Lady. But as the work proceeded and grew in elaboration, it was felt that to move so fine a piece of work to and fro, several times in the course of every year, would be to expose it to great risk of damage. It was therefore determined to make the whole Altar—with the exception, of course, of the mensa—of silver, and to fix it permanently in its place. This has now been accomplished.

"The ends of the Altar are comparatively plain. Each is divided into four panels, with moulded framing, and the panels are filled with simple designs in leaf work. The front of the Altar strikes the spectator at once by its extreme richness, and by the enormous quantity of figure-design that has been lavished upon its limited space. Eight scarf-columns project from the front surface to serve as supports for the mensa, and these columns divide the whole surface into seven spaces. Six of these spaces are further divided at half their height by a band. The seventh space — the central and somewhat larger space — is left undivided, and is filled by a niche. Compound twisted columns, with carved and jeweled bases and capitals, carry the richly cusped arch of the canopy of the niche; the spandrils above this arch are filled with open-work foliage, and the point of the arch is surmounted by a floriated crown. A diaper of fleur-de-lys, on a ground of pale blue enamel, covers the back of the niche. Within this niche stands a stately figure of Mary, holding in her arms her Child. The Holy Child grasps with one hand his Mother's robe; in the other he holds the orb of the world. It is a singularly lifelike, childlike, happy figure. The figure of the Mother is full of dignity, and especially noteworthy for the beauty of its finely modeled drapery. The twelve panels, which, with the exception of the niche, occupy the whole of the front, measure each of them seven inches by eleven and one-fourth inches. They are filled with subjects from the life of the Blessed Virgin. The series begins on the extreme left of the upper row.

"1. *The Angel's Message to St. Anne.*

St. Anne, the wife of Joachim, kneeling at a prayer-desk, receives from an angel the glad tidings that she will have a daughter, who shall bring forth the Saviour of the world.

"On the same level, to the right, we have —

"2. *The Birth of Mary.*

St. Anne is seen on a couch in the background. In the foreground are three friends, who are ministering to her child.

"On the right of this panel —

"3. *Mary's Presentation in the Temple.*

Mary, in her girlhood, is seen ascending the steps of the Temple, to which she has been led by her father and mother. In the background are the courts of the Temple, and beyond the courts a glimpse of the Mount of Olives.

"The series is now continued in the left panel of the lower row.

"4. *The Espousal of Mary and Joseph.*

In the presence of the Priest and several witnesses, Mary is betrothed to St. Joseph. A rose in full bloom stands in the foreground.

"5. *The Annunciation.*

Mary, kneeling at a richly carved prayer-desk, and with her arms crossed upon her breast, turns towards the angel who kneels near her and is holding a lily in her hand. The holy Dove hovers above Mary's head. An arcade encloses the figures, and through the arches of the arcade the trees of a garden are seen.

"6. *The Visitation.*

Mary and St. Elizabeth meet and embrace in the garden of St. Elizabeth's house. Three women stand by, gazing sympathetically at the scene. Returning to the upper row of subjects, we have, in the panel to the right of the niche, —

"7. *The Visit of the Shepherds to Bethlehem.*

In a stable thatched with straw, our Lady is seated with the divine Infant on her lap. St. Joseph is watching over her, and the shepherds have come to worship the new-born Saviour. One of them, his dog by his side, is kneeling with folded hands, and gazes at the Child.

"To the right of this we have —

"8. *The Flight into Egypt.*

Mary, seated upon an ass, holds with both arms her Child. St. Joseph, carrying provision for the way, leads the ass. In the background an angel holds up a veil to screen the Holy Family from their pursuers.

"9. *The Finding in the Temple.*

The Child Jesus is seated on the steps inside the Temple. A large book rests upon his knees, and other books lie about him. The aged priests and scribes in the background converse, wondering at the Child's questions. Mary, in trouble, expostulates, 'Son, why hast thou thus dealt with us?' and he is answering, 'Wist ye not that I must be about my Father's business?'

"The series is now continued at the lower level, where in the panel on the right of the niche we have —

"10. *The Miracle at Cana.*

In the front is the figure of the Lord; his hands are raised to bless the water that a servant is pouring into the great jars. Mary waits and watches. In the background the marriage feast is proceeding.

"11. *At the Foot of the Cross.*

Mary and the holy women sit supporting the lifeless body of the Lord, which has been lowered from the Cross. In the background the Cross is seen, and two angels are bending over the sorrowing group in worship.

"12. *The Coronation of Our Blessed Lady.*

This is the climax of the whole series. The Lord Jesus receives his Blessed Mother unto himself, that 'where he is, she may be also': and he crowns her faithfulness with 'a crown of glory that fadeth not away.' — St. John xiv. 3; Rev. ii. 10; St. Peter v. 4.

"The eight half-columns which support the Altar slab form a frame of extraordinary richness to these panels; each half-column carries on its face eighteen small niches, arranged in sets of three, one above the other, and in every niche is the figure of a saint in complete relief. These figures, 144 in number, have been separately modeled; they bear their characteristic emblems, and their names. The capitals of the columns contain, each of them, a group of three kneeling angels, some with hands clasped in prayer, and some with musical instruments. A rich band of foliage and scroll work, in deep relief, connects the capitals, and forms a supporting cornice for the mensa. Lines of roses with jeweled centres divide the lower from the upper row of subjects, and each subject from the cornice and the plinth.

"The 144 figures in the niches of the columns are arranged, with one or two slight dislocations, chronologically, beginning at the extreme right at the top with Adam, and proceeding downwards through the outer line of figures. From the lowest figure of each line, we return to the highest figure of the next line to the left, and so on. Following in consecutive order, the little figures represent the saints of the Old Testament, and the Major and Minor Prophets, passing on into the saints of the Catholic Church: but the strict sequence is interrupted in order that the saints and angels of the New Testament may stand on either side of the central figure. Then follow the confessors and martyrs; holy men and women of the later time; the great doctors of the Western Church and of the Eastern Church; the lesser theologians; the founders of religious orders, and the more conspicuous of the British missionary saints and martyrs.

"The composition as a whole, in spite of its infinity of detail, is yet a unity, and singularly compact and harmonious in effect. Over 400 jewels are distributed over the work: they are, however, so carefully placed that nowhere do they draw off attention to themselves, but are felt to add a subtle refinement and variety to the light and color which play so delightfully over the whole surface.

"When we consider how many hundreds of figures, in high and low relief, there are; the interest, variety, and beauty of the arrangement and modeling of these figures; the wealth of varied design in the decorative parts; we cannot but feel that the greatest praise is due to all concerned in the production of this remarkable Altar — artists, designers, and craftsmen. They have achieved a monumental work which does the greatest credit to them all, and which will remain as a very splendid and very delightful presentation of twentieth-century English Ecclesiastical Art.

"The figures in the niches of the columns are grouped in the following order, reading from the right to the left: —

I

"Aaron	Sarah	Adam
Joshua	Melchizedek	Eve
Samuel	Isaac	Abel
David	Jacob	Enoch
Hezekiah	Joseph	Noah
Elijah	Moses	Abraham

II

Nahum	Hosea	Elisha
Habakkuk	Joel	[Judas Maccabæus]
Zephaniah	Amos	Isaiah
Haggai	Obadiah	Jeremiah
Zechariah	Jonah	Ezekiel
Malachi	Micah	Daniel

III

St. Athanasius	St. Irenæus	St. Matthew
St. Chrysostom	St. Hilary	St. Mark
St. Basil	St. Ambrose	St. Luke
St. Gregory Naz.	St. Augustine of Hippo	St. John
Dionysius Areop.	St. Jerome	St. Justin M.
St. John of Damascus	St. Gregory the Great	St. Cyprian

IV

St. Michael	St. Peter	St. Joseph Arimath.
St. Joseph	St. Andrew	St. Stephen
St. Joachim	St. James-the-Less	St. Paul
St. Simon of Cyrene	St. Simon	St. Barnabas
St. Veronica	St. Thaddeus	St. Jude
St. Longinus	St. Matthias	St. Timothy

V

St. John Baptist	St. John Ap.	St. Gabriel
Zacharias	St. James-the-Great	St. Raphael
St. Elizabeth	St. Philip	St. Anne
St. Simeon	St. Bartholomew	St. Mary Magdalene
St. Anna	St. Thomas	St. Martha
St. Lazarus	St. Matthew	St. Mary of Bethany

VI

St. Alban	St. Ignatius M.	St. Clement Alex.
St. Denys	St. Polycarp	St. Cyril of Jerusalem
St. George	St. Clement Rom.	St. Anselm
St. Nicholas	St. Laurence	St. Bernard
St. Perpetua	St. Sebastian	St. Bonaventure
St. Cecilia	St. Vincent	St. Thomas Aquinas

VII

St. Monica	St. Catherine	St. Agnes
St. Giles	St. Boniface	St. Agatha
St. Augustin Cant.	St. Edmund K. & M.	St. Lucy
St. Patrick	St. Edward the Conf.	St. Prisca
St. David	St. Alphege	St. Faith
St. Chad	St. Martin	St. Margaret

VIII

St. Robert of Cit.	St. Helen	St. Etheldreda
St. Bruno	St. Cuthbert	V. Bede
St. Gilbert	St. Oswald	St. Swithun
St. Francis of Assisi	St. Thomas of Cant.	St. Dunstan
St. Clare	St. Anthony	St. Edmund Abp.
St. Dominic	St. Benedict	St. Hugh."

This Altar as well as the Chapel in which it is placed is a memorial to the late Mrs. Rodman Wanamaker, given by her husband.

CHURCH OF ST. JOHN THE EVANGELIST, ST. PAUL, MINN.

The Altar and Reredos were built and furnished in 1906, of quartered oak. The central compartment contains a representation of the Last Supper after Leonardo Da Vinci. The figures on the right and left indicate adoring angels. The work was designed and built by the American Seating Company in their Manitowoc Wisconsin shops. The cost was about $2500. The Altar and Reredos are Memorials to the late Mrs. Fanny S. Wilder of St. Paul.

ALTAR AND REREDOS IN THE CHURCH OF ST. JOHN THE EVANGELIST, ST. PAUL, MINN.

INDEX

Aldenham, Lord, 45; quoted, 46.
Allen, F. R., 306.
All Saints' Cathedral, Milwaukee, 239.
All Saints' Church, Evesham, 221; Richard's Castle, 227; Dorchester, 312.
American Seating Company, 356.
Armstead, H., 74.
Atkinson and Mylhertz, 288.
Aumonier, W., 156.

Bacon Bros., 122.
Bailey and Bassett, 278.
Beall, R. S., 62.
Beverley Minster, 161.
Bitter, K., 365.
Blashfield, E. H., 283.
Blomfield, Sir A. W., 102, 111.
Bodley, Sir G. F., 55, 85, 92, 115, 181.
Bodley and Garner, 66, 79.
Borgia Bros., 254.
Boulton, R. L., 40, 221.
Boulton and Sons, 151.
Bridgeman, H., 85, 181.
Bridges, Mr., 215.
Brielmaier and Sons, 239.
Brightman, Rev. F. E., quoted, 134.
Brindley, Mr., 55.
Bristol Cathedral, 50.
Buckeridge, C. E., 106, 227.
Buckeridge and Floyce, 111.
Bucknall and Comper, 116.
Burford Church, 203.
Burlison and Grylls, 122.

Cappelli, E., 278.
Cathedral of St. Alban, 45; St. John the Divine, New York, 233; Quincy, Ill., 240; St. Nicholas, Newcastle-on-Tyne, 62.
Chapel of All Souls' College, Oxford, 133; Cheltenham College, 151; Jesus College, Oxford, 128; Marlborough College, 127; Magdalen College, 134; New College, 139; St. John's College, Hurstpierpont, 145; Winchester College, 140; St. Paul's School, Concord, 330.
Chester Cathedral, 49.
Chichester Cathedral, 61.
Christ Church, Bristol, 186; Reading, 228; New Haven, 317.
Christ Church Cathedral, Oxford, 55; Louisville, 234.

Christ Church Priory, 170.
Church of the Advent, Boston, 311; Ascension, Chicago, 355; Epiphany, Washington, 300; Holy Redeemer, London, 86; Holy Trinity, Middletown, 318; Incarnation, New York, 260; the Saviour, Philadelphia, 283; St. Alban, London, 79; St. John the Divine, London, 91; St. Edward the Martyr, New York, 265; St. Ignatius, New York, 259; St. Mary Magdalene, Elmstone, 182; St. Michael and All Angels, Anniston, 343; Transfiguration, 254; Zion and St. Timothy, New York, 266; St. John the Evangelist, St. Paul, 378.
Champneys, B., 34.
Chandler, T. P., 294.
Clarke, S., 61.
Clayton and Bell, 209, 330.
Coleman, C., 361.
Congdon, H. M., 234, 299, 329, 350.
Convent of St. Margaret, East Grinstead, 175; St. Mary, Peekskill, 350; Nativity, Fond du Lac, 356.
Cottingham, Jr., Mr., 40.
Cottingham, L. N., 134.
Coxe Sons and Vining, 318.
Cram, Goodhue, and Ferguson, 244, 272, 312.

Davison, R., 39.
Durham Cathedral, 56.

Earp, Mr., 197.
Earp and Hobbs, 175, 198.
Eden, Rev. R. A., quoted, 111.
Ellin and Kitson, 250, 253.
Elwell, Mr., 96.
Ely Cathedral, 3.
Emmanuel Church, Boston, 306.
Endolithic Marble Co., 338, 361.
Evans and Co., 260, 306, 312, 317.
Evans and Tombs, 337.
Exeter Cathedral, 13.

Farmer and Brindley, 2, 8, 25, 33, 49, 79, 91, 96, 121, 139.
Field, Mr., 7.
Fisher, R. C., 271.
Fisher and Bird, 259.
Forsythe, J., 102, 148.
Fowler, H., 19.

Gardner, Rev. Canon, quoted, 26.
Geflowski, G. E., 133, 210, 215.

Geissler, R., 265, 266, 305.
General Theological Seminary, New York, 271.
Gilbert, A., 45.
Gloucester Cathedral, 14.
Godwin, Mr., 192
Gorham Co., 323.
Grace Church, Baltimore, 299; Windsor, 323; Utica, 365.
Grant, Miss, 95.
Gruhler, W. J., 294.

Haight, C. C., 271, 318.
Hardman and Sons, 288.
Hardman and Co., J., 336.
Heaton, Butler, and Bayne, 198, 228, 323.
Hedley, R., 122.
Hems, H., 45.
Hereford Cathedral, 40.
Hewitt, G. W. and W. D., 288.
Hicks and Charlewood, 122.
Hirst, H., 30, 191.
Hitch, N., 30, 139, 161, 164, 222.
Holiday, H., 277.
Holy Trinity Church, Watermoor, 215; Middletown, 318.
Hudson, Mr., 7.
Hughes, J. F., 365.

Irving and Casson, 330, 337.

Johnson, R. J., 62.

Kempe, C. E., 33.

Lamb, J. and R., 265.
Leonardi, 287.
Lichfield Cathedral, 33.

Manchester Cathedral, 34.
Minster Lovell, 204.
Moore, T. L., 96.
Mora, Mr., 306, 312.

Neville Screen, 56.
Nicholls, T., 209, 228.
Nolloth, D.D., Rev. Canon, quoted, 161.
Norcross Bros., 324.
Norman and Burt, 61.
Nowell, D.D., Rev. Canon W. E., quoted, 122.

Oertel, D.D., Rev. J. A., 244.
Old St. Pancras Church, London, 111.
Ostrehan, G., 176.

Partridge, W. O., 300.
Pearson, G. T., 293, 349.
Pearson, J. L., 30, 50, 139, 164, 222.
Penrose, G. T., 164.

Perkins, Rev. T., quoted, 170.
Peterborough Cathedral, 39.
Peto, H., 311.
Philips, B., 228.
Phillips, J., 7.
Pomeroy and Cay, 86.
Poole and Allen, 148.
Potter, W. A., 324.
Powell, Messrs., 85, 191.
Prothero, H. A., 151.
Purdy, E., 221.

Randall, H., 300.
Ratte, Mr., 4.
Rede, D.D., Rev. W., quoted, 240.
Redfern, Mr., 14.
Rhind, J. M., 318.
Rice, Mr., 192.
Rider, J., 86.
Robertson, C. G., quoted, 133.
Rochester Cathedral, 19.
Rose, P. C., 244.
Ross and Co., 244.
Rubicondi, 287.

St. Agnes' Church, London, 96.
St. Alban's Church, London, 79.
St. Anne's Church, Eastbourne, 116.
St. Barnabas Church, London, 101.
St. Chad's Church, Haggerston, 197.
St. Cuthbert's Church, Newcastle-on-Tyne, 122.
St. Elizabeth's Church, Philadelphia, 278.
St. George's Chapel, Windsor, 155.
St. Giles' Church, London, 106.
St. Ignatius' Church, New York, 259.
St. James' Church, Philadelphia, 272.
St. John Baptist Church, Cirencester, 210; Summertown, 216.
St. John's Church, Dresden, 366; London, 91, 102; Stamford, 324.
St. Luke's Church, Germantown, 293; Scranton, 344.
St. Margaret's Church, King's Lynn, 181.
St. Mary Magdalene, Elmstone, 182.
St. Mary's Church, Bristol, 192; Cuddington, 121; Marsh Gibbon, 198; Kansas City, 361; Primrose Hill, London, 115; Soho, London, 95; Streatley, 222; Philadelphia, 287; Witney, 209.
St. Matthew's Church, Northampton, 156.
St. Michael and All Angels Church, Anniston, 343.
St. Paul's Cathedral, London, 66.
St. Paul's Church, Bristol, 191; Chattanooga, 338; London, 80; Washington, 305.
St. Paul's School, Concord, 330.
St. Peter's Church, Germantown, 294.
St. Stephen's Church, Clewer, 176; London, 85; Philadelphia, 277; Providence, 335.

INDEX

St. Timothy's Church, Philadelphia, 288.
Salisbury Cathedral, 8.
Salviati, 49, 74, 355.
Schweichart, Mr., 323.
Scott, Sir G. G., 4, 8, 13, 14, 19, 25, 33, 49, 74, 96, 139, 155, 210, 215.
Sedding, J. D., 86.
Sergeant, P. W., quoted, 1.
Sharpless and Watts, 278.
Shaw, N., 227.
Sibbel, J., 350.
Silver Altar of St. Mark's Church, Philadelphia, 371.
Smith, J., 324.
Southwark Cathedral, London, 70.
Staller, H., 115.
Stent, E. J. N., 355.
Stewart and Hendry, 343.
Street, G. E., 20, 95, 128, 203.
Sturgis, J. H., 311.

Theis' Sons, P., 329.
Thomas, J. A., 121.
Thompson, D.D., Rev. Canon, quoted, 70.
Thornhill, Sir J., 133.
Tiffany, L. C., 233, 344.
Tinworth, Mr., 20.
Trinity Church, Geneva, 349; New York, 247; Torrington, 329.

Trinity Chapel, New York, 253.
Truro Cathedral, 26.
Tully, J. C., 259.

Upjohn, R. M., 365.

Valenzi, 287.
Vauchet, F., 50.
Vaughan, H., 260, 317, 330, 337.

Wall, A. B., 185.
Watts, R., 336.
West, Sir B., 2, 19.
Westmacott, J. S., 62.
Westminster Abbey, 74.
Wheeler Bros., 228.
Whitman Company, 293, 349.
Winchester Cathedral, 1 ; College, 140.
Withers, F. C., 247, 253, 254.
Withers, R. H., 80.
Wood, W. H., 266, 338, 343.
Woodyear, H., 176, 228.
Worcester Cathedral, 25.
Wyatt, T., 128.

York Cathedral, 20.

www.ingramcontent.com/pod-product-compliance
Lightning Source LLC
Chambersburg PA
CBHW060505300426
44112CB00017B/2559